For Donna,

An early Birthday gift—
"Romancing" well into your 8Th
Decade. Our admiration and love,

Sally and Judy

ROMANCING

GREEN, Henry; Managing Director of Engineering Co., Birmingham; *b* 1905; *m* 1929; one *s. Educ:* Public Sch; Oxford Univ. Engineer in Food and Drink Trade; War of 1939–45, full time NFS (in the ranks), 1939–43. *Publications:* Blindness, 1926; Living, 1929; Party Going, 1939; Pack My Bag, 1940; Caught, 1943; Loving, 1945; Back, 1946; Concluding, 1948; Nothing, 1950; Doting, 1952 . . . *Recreation:* romancing over the bottle, to a good band . . .

Who's Who, 1973

ROMANCING

THE LIFE AND WORK OF HENRY GREEN

Jeremy Treglown

RANDOM HOUSE NEW YORK

All rights reserved under International and Pan-American Copyright Conventions.
Published in the United States by Random House, Inc., New York, and simultaneously
in Canada by Random House of Canada Limited, Toronto.

Random House and colophon are registered trademarks of Random House, Inc.

This work was originally published in Great Britain by Faber and Faber Limited in 2000.

Library of Congress Cataloging-in-Publication Data

Treglown, Jeremy.
Romancing : the life and work of Henry Green / Jeremy Treglown.
p. cm.
Includes bibliographical references and index.
ISBN 0-679-43303-1 (acid-free paper)
1. Green, Henry, 1905–1974.   2. Literature and society—English—History—
20th century.   3. Aristocracy (Social class)—Great Britain—Biography.
4. Novelists, English—20th century—Biography.   5. Social classes in literature.
I. Title.

PR6013.R416 Z89 2001
823′.912—dc21
[B]   00-055307

Owing to limitations of space, acknowledgments of permission to
reprint published and unpublished material appear on p. 318.

Random House website address: www.atrandom.com

Printed in the United States of America on acid-free paper

2 4 6 8 9 7 5 3

First U.S. Edition

Book design by Barbara M. Bachman

To Beryl Treglown

and in memory of

Geoffrey Treglown

HENRY GREEN'S BOOKS ARE ROMANTIC CREATIONS, yet they are also "true"—not least in sometimes incorporating real-life characters and situations.[1] This is a pitfall for a biographer. Fictions, including fictions of self, can be diminished too easily by being translated back into the prosaic language of facts, even in the rare cases where the facts are unambiguous. In this first biography of the novelist, I give some illustrations of how Henry Green deployed the specifics of Henry Yorke's experience, but for the most part my account of the life is linked to the books more in terms of moods and thematic preoccupations and of the influence of the practicalities of publishing and critical reception. I make no apology for describing the novels in some detail: They are the biography's main raison d'être. But a biography is what it is, and not everything in it is directly related to Green's writing. Green himself criticized Leonard Woolf for editing the more personal elements out of Virginia Woolf's journals: "Most of us, as she was, are incurably curious," this by then reclusive and always paradoxical man wrote in his 1954 review of *A Writer's Diary*.[2] "And when we are concerned with one of the great women of our time, it is hard to be denied." The denial made him wish for a full account of Woolf's life. As far as Green's own life is concerned, this is just one account. Some kinds of family tenderness and discretion can last for generations, and even when questions of custody and access do not significantly arise, biography is a form whose subjectivity (no one's view of a person is the same as another's) can in the end be overcome only by dialogue. A life of Henry Green was needed, but so, now, is another one.

An area in which no one can do the right thing by him is nomenclature, about which, as will become clear in chapter 1, his feelings were intricate even by his own standards. I at first wanted to use "Green" for the writer and "Yorke" for the industrialist and family man, but this posed problems: The two are far from always distinct, and in the latter case there are inevitably many contexts in which several Yorkes figure. Most people who knew him well just refer to "Henry," as if there could be no question whom they mean, and—pulled along, too, by the tide of usage under which surnames are fast disappearing—I have often found myself presuming to do the same. The alternative would have been to refer to him in the anonymous fashion that he sometimes favored in his books as this man, this unignorable author.

VICTORIA GLENDINNING, IN A CONVERSATION ABOUT novels set in the Second World War, first recommended *Caught* to me in 1989. I had not read anything by Henry Green, an ignorance that I put right over the following weeks. In the wartime phrase Eudora Welty was to use when telling me about her own first encounter with him, it was "a direct hit."

As I was to discover, a less fruitful kind of embattlement had characterized some aspects of Green's posthumous career. (He died in 1973.) Established authors either had approached the family asking to write a biography and been refused or were themselves approached about it and for one reason or another declined. For several years, the novelist Paul Bailey was authorized to write a life, but the unfinished project ended in acrimony. At the end of 1989, I somewhat impulsively offered to take on the job. Green's executor, his son, Sebastian Yorke, turned me down. Soon afterward, Christopher Maclehose of Harvill Press (then Collins Harvill) undertook to bring out all of Green's novels in paperback, and I was commissioned to write the introductions. Because these pieces were to have biographical as well as critical dimensions, I was given access to the extensive archive of manuscripts and correspondence, including copies of letters by Green, that Sebastian Yorke had brought together at his house in rural North Yorkshire. Some of these—notably, early drafts of several of the novels—had previously been on loan to the British Library, where scholars had been able to read them at their leisure, but they had been withdrawn after the death of Green's widow, Dig, in 1985.

Late in 1991, when the first of the Harvill reissues appeared, Sebastian Yorke formally, though as it was to turn out briefly, authorized me to write a biography. At a time when literary biographies were getting bad press, in some cases rightly, inevitable disagreements over aspects of content and emphasis loomed larger than they might otherwise have, and after about a year Yorke withdrew his authorization. However, he continued to be very helpful with my introductions to the novels, as well as with other pieces that I wrote about his father, especially a long biographical article published in *The New Yorker* in 1993. Although I fully recognized how complex and strong Sebastian Yorke's feelings about a full biography were, my own not unambivalent view was and is that, however understandably, they were getting in the way of a wider readership for Henry Green and that it was in the interests of Green's work that I persevere. Such issues have never been uncontroversial, and readers will form their own opinions. Meanwhile, I thank Sebastian Yorke for the assistance that he and his wife gave me during the first four years of my research.

Because this book is unauthorized, a few doors remain closed to me, among them those of Green's cousin Francis Wyndham and of a small number of Green's other friends or their descendants, including his niece Princess Loewenstein (who nonetheless commented helpfully on a draft). But many of his surviving friends and relations helped me a great deal. I owe special thanks to Alice Keene, to Lucy Butler, Sir Raymond and Lady Carr, Kitty and Wynne Godley, Hidé Ishiguro, Venetia Murray, the late Anthony Powell and Lady Violet Powell, the late Alan Pryce-Jones, Alan Ross, Carol Southern and the late Terry Southern, the late Sir Stephen Spender, Emma Tennant, Eudora Welty, John Yorke, and to Paul Bailey. Most of these people saw me more than once, some allowing me to read relevant letters and other papers in their possession, and some commenting on the book in draft.

I am grateful to have had access to the papers of Nevill Coghill at Eton; of John Lehmann at Austin, Texas, and at Princeton; and of Rosamond Lehmann at King's College, Cambridge; as well as to the archives of the Hogarth Press and to the BBC Written Archives. In the Further Acknowledgments on pp. 317–18 I mention other debts to archivists, librarians, people who met Henry Yorke or had access to information concerning him, and many others who have given occasional guidance or encouragement. I also acknowledge there the owners of copyrights in materials from which I have quoted.

The book was written with all kinds of readers in mind, as long as they are readers or potential readers of Henry Green, so I do not engage with every nuance of disagreement among academic specialists. But I have benefited from their work, especially from Rod Mengham's brilliant if sometimes overingenious critical study, *The Idiom of the Time: The Writings of Henry Green,* and Ann Hancock's 1981 Ph.D. dissertation, in the course of preparing which she corresponded with a number of Green's friends, some of whom, notably Harold Acton and Goronwy Rees, had either died by the time I began my own research or died during the course of it. Details of these and other works that I have found helpful can be found in the notes and in the Select Bibliography.

Jean Stein, editor of *Grand Street,* and Harold Evans, then president of Random House, provided much-needed support in the early stages; Tina Brown and some of her *New Yorker* colleagues, particularly Kim Heron, helped farther along the way; and the University of Warwick granted me a sabbatical, on which the book was completed. My agent, Deborah Rogers, and my editors, Julian Loose at Faber and Faber and Daniel Menaker at Random House, as well as Christopher Maclehose and Guido Waldman at Harvill, have been unfailingly encouraging. I have particular debts to two old friends and mentors: Stephen Wall (who in addition to his criticism and novels has written a stage version of *Loving*) for his detailed comments on the first draft; and Karl Miller for help of many kinds. The person I have most reason to thank, though, is the one who amid all her support has with her usual forthrightness expressed more—and more fundamental—doubts and criticisms than I have always been grateful to hear: my wife, Holly.

CONTENTS

ROMANCING

CHAPTER 1

Names

THE RIVER SEVERN MEANDERS AROUND THE YORKE estate in Gloucestershire, between Forthampton Court, the big old house where one member of the family still lives, and the abbey town of Tewkesbury. On sleepy summer evenings in the 1910s, Vincent and Maud Yorke's youngest son, Henry, would sit in a boat fishing, a safe distance from his intimidatingly energetic and clever elder brothers and a few yards from workingmen who had cycled out from the town to fish from the meadow bank opposite. He imagined, as he later wrote, that between him and the men "there was something conspiratorial . . . hunched over our floats as shadows began to stretch out long over the surface of the water." The other thing he liked about the activity was the "exciting connection with a remote element when there is only a hint of what is going on. . . . Not being able to see but only to feel."[1]

In this memory, with its outsider's attraction to the lives of other people and its relish for intuition rather than knowledge, suggestion rather than explicitness, lies the embryo of a unique novelist who, in the intervals of his job as a not very successful businessman, was to write at lunchtimes and in the evenings under the name Henry Green. *Loving,* Green's 1945 novel about the servants in a big country house in neutral Ireland during the Second World War, includes a vivid scene centered on a game of blindman's buff, in which you have to feel people in order to tell who they are. "Not being able to see" was the subject of his first book, *Blindness,* begun when he was still in school and published before he left university. The romantic plight of the newly sightless central character, a thinly disguised version of the author, enables him to hear those around him better, giving him access to not only their words but also their thoughts. As the Southern American writer Eudora Welty was to put it, Henry Green turned what people say "into the fantasy of what they are telling each other, at the same time calling up out of their mouths their vital spirit."[2]

In the middle of the twentieth century, anyone in the literary world on either side of the Atlantic who was asked to list the most important living writers in the English language would have immediately thought of Henry Green. Today, almost fifty years after the publication of the last of his novels, Green should be ranked among the great modern novelists, those whom James Wood has called "the last true magi of language." Wood rightly claims that in England, Green is the greatest of them after D. H. Lawrence and Virginia Woolf.[3] The most obvious difference between him and them, of course, is the blankness that comes over most people's faces today when his name is mentioned. Yet he has never lacked articulate admirers. To John Updike he "brings the rectangle of printed page alive like little else in English fiction of this century."[4] V. S. Pritchett wrote of him as "a spirit of poetry, fantasy and often wild laughter, an original."[5] Eudora Welty said that his imagination was "the most interesting and vital . . . in English fiction in our time,"[6] and to the young John Ashbery he stood alone in combining prose-poetry with fidelity to everyday life, "the Cordelia of modern novelists."[7] So why, outside professional literary circles, has he been almost unknown?

In a famous interview for *The Paris Review*, the Beat novelist Terry Southern said that there are writers and writer's writers, but that Henry Green was a writer's writer's writer. To the extent that this suggests that he isn't a reader's writer, it's misleading; but like any serious artist, he needs a climate not only of respect but of broad understanding in which to be appreciated, and that has been missing. Part of the problem has been the lack of a biography—the only popular form of literary history in Western culture. Another difficulty is Green's individuality. There are ways in which he can be compared with his peers: not only with Lawrence and Woolf but with Kafka, Gertrude Stein, William Faulkner. But what is most important about him is how unlike anyone else he is.

Green's is an intuitive, oblique, often wayward kind of art. In the

1920s, when his publisher wanted "society" novels, Green wrote about industrial Birmingham. In the 1950s, when working-class topics became popular, he set his books in the exclusive, fast-fading milieu depicted by Ivy Compton-Burnett and Noël Coward. All of his novels are electric with sex, but he never comes near to describing the act. Green's bright young things on an outing to France get no farther than Victoria Station; his Second World War firefighters are furtive, lustful slackers rather than heroes. He sees life in terms of bathos, at its most surprising and poetic when it is most mundane, and partly for this reason the novels are, among much else, exceptionally funny. And while they can make you laugh out loud when you least expect to, they also exhibit a gratuitous stylistic bravura, splashing on color as in fauvist paintings. The novels' refusal of congruity or appropriateness has a lot to do with instincts— the instincts of characters and also Green's writerly instincts about truth and about effect—overriding any preconceived notions of what should happen in a novel, or in life. These qualities are among those that place Green's books among the outstanding romantic (as well as modernist) novels of his century, though not in a way that easily fits the stereotypes of romance.

Like Henry Green, Henry Yorke, too, was a romantic. He prized feeling much more than judgment and was always searching, though in more traditional ways than in the books, for other worlds of possibility. The fact, which he insisted on only half-jokingly, that he was an aristocrat has a bearing on his work, as does the fact that he was an industrialist. In being these and a major novelist, he was unique in English literary history. The complex personality of Henry Yorke and the connections both clear and missing between him and Henry Green are fascinating in themselves and also unusually revealing about the psychology of art—not least because in a century of self-publicity, he himself was one of the causes of his neglect, through his extreme, though far from straightforward, reticence.

IN THE ALMANAC OF THE BRITISH ESTABLISHMENT, *Who's Who*, every person listed writes his or her own entry within a set format. Henry Green first appeared in the 1948 volume, when he was forty-three and had already published seven of his ten books. There was no reference to him under Yorke, "family name of Earl of Hardwicke," where details appear about Henry's father, Vincent, a landowner and rich businessman; his uncle Ralph, who was a general; and his distant cousin Simon Yorke, the eccentric, reclusive owner of Erddig, in North Wales. Nor was there a cross-reference from Yorke to Henry Green, whose entry is for the most part painstakingly uninformative. He is described as the managing director of an unnamed engineering company in Birmingham. He has been educated at a public school, also unnamed, and at an unidentified college at Oxford. He reveals that he married in 1929 but doesn't say who his wife is. The address given is that of his publisher, not his home. The titles of his books, on the other hand, are listed in full. And, as if to make up for his earlier secretiveness, under the optional category "Recreation," where his father conventionally recorded "hunting and shooting" and many others chose to say nothing, Green suddenly confessed, "romancing over the bottle, to a good band."

This item in *Who's Who* remained unchanged, except for the addition of subsequent book titles, until Green's death. In miniature, it typifies an important dimension of his approach to being a writer. Much of his fiction was in one way or another recognizably, deeply autobiographical—"true," as he told his later editor, John Lehmann, about one of his short stories set in the Blitz.[8] Yet he never wrote under his real name, would not let his publishers distribute biographical information about him, and disliked being photographed unless all that was seen, as in Magritte's portrait of the surrealist Edward James, was the back of his head. He was inconsistent in these, as in most, matters: He gave a few interviews, allowed some conventional photographs. But it was as if, for him, a condition of telling the truth, however imaginatively, was the fantasy that the author could remain unknown, that his books would be read in the dark. He was at bottom a shy man, in some respects very low in self-esteem, and one face of his self-effacement was that he put others into the foreground, creating fictional people out of existing ones and giving them new names.

Who people were mattered very much to his family, but the taxonomy it employed was the traditional one of class, kin, and ancestry. Henry Yorke countered these obsessions by turning them into various aspects of their reverse: affectionate satire on upper-class life, for example, combined with a modernist passion for the present day and for the lives of apparently insignificant people. Yet some of the roots of his fiction inevitably lie deep in his family background—a fact that may have come home to him when the completion of *Blindness* in 1925 coincided with the publication of a biography of an eighteenth-century ancestress, Isabelle de Charrière ("Belle de Zuylen").[9] She was the daughter of Baron van Tuyll van Seeroskerken, head of a Dutch family celebrated for, among other things, its sense of its own importance. Under the disguises of pseudonymous narrators and letter writers, most famously Zélide in *The Portrait of Zélide*, Mme. de Charrière freed herself to satirize her world and its constraints derived from gender and class.

To her young descendant, pseudonyms and anonymity were in themselves imaginatively important. When he began to publish stories at school, he called himself Henry Michaels. On the original typescript of *Blindness* he became Henry Browne. Finally, to the regret of his friend Harold Acton, he settled for Green. (Acton saw the pseudonym as little more revealing than outright anonymity: "There are Greens of so many shades writing novels that one wishes he had selected another colour.")[10] But however conventional and superficial-seeming such dissimulations have been for many writers, in Green's case they were unusually pervasive. In his interim memoir, *Pack My Bag,* he says: "Names distract, nicknames are too easy and if leaving both out . . . makes a book look blind then that to my mind is no disadvantage." What would it mean for a book to be blind? That it couldn't read you, perhaps, and in Henry Green more than in most writers there was a deep argument going on between self-revelation and secrecy.

At one level, he simply feared the disapproval of his crushingly grand relations. A century after Isabelle's time, another van Tuyll married John Reginald Yorke, a prosperous Gloucestershire landowner and member of Parliament. In 1899, their brilliant, rather austere elder son, Vincent, married the vivacious Maud Wyndham, whose father was the second Baron Leconfield—among the richest members of the British aristocracy and owner of one of the most magnificent houses in England: Petworth, in Sussex.[11] During Henry's childhood, Petworth was a kind of reserve not only for its famous collections but for almost any relic of traditional values. Even after the First World War, male guests there were always expected to wear white tie and tails at dinner. When, as sometimes happened, one of them had to apologize for having brought nothing more formal than a dinner jacket, their host would advise, "You should sack your man," as if valets were not becoming rarer than tailcoats.[12] Henry's mother, Maud, was no less imperious. One of the stories told most often about her is that she offended her gardener, Poole, by making him bowl turnips out the French windows and down a grass slope, so that she could shoot at them. According to the legend, she called Poole "Gardener"—"Gardener, gardener, I'm going to shoot!"—but in *Pack My Bag*, Henry defensively insists that she used his surname.[13] If one part of his feeling about names came from shyness, another, related part had to do with asserting the identities of others: naming the supposedly anonymous. The opening of his second book, *Living*, published when Green was in his mid-twenties and based on his experiences of his family's Birmingham foundry, introduces by name twenty-six workingmen and -women in as many pages. In *Party Going*, the comically shifting relationships between the rich socialites at the center of the story are set in an ironic context by the attention the narrative pays to their numerous long-suffering servants, most of whom are identified scrupulously. There is a natural progression from this to *Loving*, where the servants in a big country house take over the story at the expense (literally) of their grand employers.

The origins of these concerns can be traced back to Henry's watchful childhood observation of servants and other staff and how they were treated. In a protoabsurdist vignette about life at Petworth, probably written during a school holiday there, he fantasizes about how his mother's family might behave if a giant appeared on the grounds. The first step taken by Maud's brother Charles, the third Lord Leconfield, is to send the butler, Wickham, to tell the intruder to go away.[14] The giant throws the butler into the lake, whereupon Charles delivers the perfunctory encomium, "Wickham was a good servant." It soon becomes clear, however, that since Wickham was carrying the keys to the cellar, one of the family's escape routes has been lost, at which Charles's piety quickly gives way to irritation about the impossibility, however often you tell them, of persuading servants to leave keys on an accessible hook.

Maud was a busy but affectionate mother, almost as devoted to her sons as to her horses and dogs. Her first child, Philip, was born in 1900, when she was twenty-six, Gerald a year later, Henry (named after Maud's father) in 1905. Henry remembered her asking him, "How much do you love me—more than toffee?" and "More than this much?" putting her thumb and forefinger together.[15] This was in the precious single hour that he spent with her between five and six each evening, once his older brothers had gone away to school. The rest of the time he was looked after by a nanny and other servants, who took him on walks and taught him to eat politely—"left hand on one's lap and the other putting not too much in at a time,"[16]—while Maud, like most of her relations, gave herself energetically to country pursuits: horses, dogs, the church, the village. Henry, who later attributed his neuroticism to her having ridden "across fences" until two months before his birth, included many aspects of her in the character of Emily Haye in *Blindness* and dedicated the book "To my mother."[17] If Mrs. Haye writes, she uses an inkstand made from a favorite horse's hoof. If she reads, it is about hunting ("This book was interestin', she had never known that the Bolton had distemper in '08 and mange in '09, a most awkward time for them, and the bitch pack had been practically annihilated").[18] The Oxford don Maurice Bowra was to say that Maud's diction was so grand that she even managed to leave the *g*s out of words that didn't contain them, "such as Cheltin'ham and Chippin'ham."[19] Small and slightly humpbacked, a chain-smoker of Turkish cigarettes, a voracious reader and a shrewd gossip, she had an unexpectedly self-deprecating wit. When she had finished what she called her "morning battle" with the newspaper, she would complain, "It's so much bigger than me."

She seems to have felt that her children, too, were in some ways bigger than she was. She had had no formal education and for all her intelligence and personal strength feared the day when each of the boys was to be sent off to school. "You were a lovely baby when you were small," Mrs. Haye tells her stepson in *Blindness*, "and I could do everything for you then, and I loved it. But now you've outgrown me in a way and left me behind."[20] But this idea of the boy's superiority isn't confirmed in the book's presentation of Emily Haye. There is plenty of affectionate comedy at the expense of her "county" values, perhaps most memorably when the newly blinded John in a vulnerable moment asks her to describe his long-dead father and she replies, "Dear boy, he was the finest man to hounds in three counties, and the most lovely shot. I remember him killing fifty birds in sixty cartridges with driven grouse at your grandfather's up in Scotland. A beautiful shot. He would have helped."[21]

But Emily is a strong, loyal, and practical woman: the most attractive person in the book.

Maud Wyndham's family had figured in public life since the Middle Ages. There was an artistic dimension to its knack for acquiring wealth and power. Maud's great-grandfather, the third earl of Egremont, for example, was a hospitable and discriminating if not entirely unself-interested patron who gave J. M. W. Turner a studio at the start of his career and was also a generous friend of John Constable, John Flaxman, and other artists, some of whose works can be seen at Petworth now, though the house was closed to the public when Henry was young. (He complained to a friend that his uncle had this "enormous collection of china, pictures etc. at Petworth and . . . *absolutely refuses* to let anyone see it ever": hence, perhaps, his pleasure in the idea of Petworth being invaded by a giant.)[22] When Maud was twenty, one of her uncles, Lord Rosebery, was prime minister. The next prime minister but three, Herbert Henry Asquith, married her cousin, Margot Tennant. It wasn't for nothing that a nephew of Maud's, John Wyndham (later Lord Egremont), private secretary to Harold Macmillan, gave his autobiography the title *Wyndham and Children First.* In the words of one of Henry's earliest friends, the novelist Anthony Powell, "the Wyndhams think the most tremendous amount of themselves."[23] The impression was reinforced by their sheer numbers. Maud was one of nine children. Henry could hardly speak the word *aunt* without shuddering.

Everyone recognized Maud in Henry's first novel. As for her husband, Vincent Yorke, the most important point about the fictional father in *Blindness* is that he is dead. So much so that there's some uncertainty about his name: Emily calls him Ralph, but the elderly nanny remembers him as Richard.[24]

Yorke was a less famous name than Wyndham, but the family was little less formidable. Forthampton Court, like Petworth House, is full of memorabilia—portraits of ancestors, books about them, things that belonged to them. The very structure of the place speaks of these forebears, through the architectural changes made to the medieval mansion by generation after generation, ever since James Yorke, an eighteenth-century bishop, married Mary Maddox, daughter and heir of the bishop of Worcester, then the owner of the house and its thousand-acre estate. Forthampton Court is one of those houses that represent every period and none—a fourteenth-century manor with a great hall, successively added to by its occupiers, among them the pre-Reformation abbots of Tewkesbury.

Before his marriage, James Yorke was not a man of property, although he had been brought up in a house more splendid than Forthampton, Wimpole Hall in Cambridgeshire. Wimpole was bought in 1739 by James's powerful father, Philip, who had recently become lord chancellor and was to be given the title Earl of Hardwicke. Although very wealthy, he was notoriously careful with money, and James, the fifth son, had to fend for himself.[25] Meanwhile, his elder brother Philip, eventually the second earl, married Jemima, Marchioness Grey, and devoted himself to improving Wimpole and particularly to building up its library—he was a bibliophile and one of the founding fathers of the British Museum. His heir, also named Philip, was the first viceroy of Ireland after the Union and a patron of several great artists and designers, among them the architect John Soane. At Hamels, in Hertfordshire, Soane designed a Marie Antoinettish dairy-cum–sitting room for Philip Yorke's wife, an exercise in the vogue for rustic sublimity that was to be parodied in *Loving*.[26]

The Forthampton branch of the Yorke family also flourished in its way. In Henry's infancy, Forthampton Court was still lived in by his grandfather, John Reginald Yorke, great-grandson of the bishop, by now a white-bearded old man whom Henry remembered pottering about the village, poking with his stick at any litter he found.[27] Vincent, Maud, and the boys were in a large L-shaped house known whimsically as "The Cottage," about a mile away on the estate. John Reginald Yorke's marriage to Sophie van Tuyll was his second. (Both his first wife and their son, Augustus, had died, the latter having set fire to his nightshirt with a candle after a drunken party.)[28] He was not only the local member of Parliament but an intellectual and something of an artist. He took a practical interest in progressive, socially reformist ideas, commissioning William Burges to build a row of almshouses behind Forthampton's parish church (which he also restored), in place of the earlier workhouse. He was an early patron of the Arts and Crafts movement, hiring Philip Webb to redesign parts of Forthampton Court with a large-scale simplicity that unites the building's spasmodic magnificence with its more rambling, farmhouse-like elements. And he was a skilled photographer whose subjects included the villagers and estate workers. He shared this enthusiasm with the Yorkes of Erddig, who for several generations since the mid-eighteenth century had commissioned portraits and, eventually, photographs of their servants and written affectionate light verse about them.[29]

This attraction to "ordinary" people anticipated strong elements in Henry's imaginative makeup. And although his father insisted that none of his forebears had been a writer (which was a way of saying that he didn't think his son should be one), Vincent had forgotten two gifted women. When Bishop Yorke was in his distant diocese, his wife, Mary, wrote him vivid letters that have proved to be a valuable source for local historians. And, as we have seen, there was Mary's Dutch contemporary, Isabelle de Charrière.[30] Neither Isabelle nor any of Henry's other ancestors is referred to in *Pack My Bag,* except obliquely in the book's famously choked, elliptical opening words, "I was born a mouthbreather with a silver spoon in 1905." But Maud figures importantly, and Vincent is an awesome presence in the background, prompting a mixture of respect and hesitancy the moment he briefly appears: "We were well brought up and saw our parents twice a day, that is to say my father worked in London and we only saw him at weekends." Vincent Yorke was in his mid-thirties when Henry was born. As a young man, Vincent was thought very handsome (the future novelist E. F. Benson had an agonizingly unrequited—and possibly quite unnoticed—crush on him when they shared rooms at Cambridge).[31] In later portraits, bespectacled, solidly built, with his hands folded complacently in front of him, he looks like a bank manager—which, among other things and in an exalted sense, he soon was: a director of the Bank of Scotland and of what was then the Westminster Bank, and also of a big insurance company, as well as chairman of the lucrative Mexican Railway.[32] His powerful City career had begun with his marriage, when he took over a near-bankrupt business in Holborn and made it profitable. Until then, he had been an archaeologist and something of an explorer, and this multiple life both reflected the divisions in his own father and was passed on in quite different forms to his sons. Henry was to take it as axiomatic that people lived at least "two lives with two sets of values."[33]

Vincent's career was almost bound to have been split. He was formidably versatile. He had won scholarships both at Eton and at King's College, Cambridge, where he took a double First in classics and became a Fellow, pursuing research into the ancient archaeology of Greece and the Near East. Physically very fit—he played real tennis for the university and once turned out for the Gloucestershire cricket team captained by W. G. Grace—he thrived on arduous expeditions.[34] On one of these, he and a friend explored previously unmapped Kurdish-occupied territory between the Mediterranean and the Black Sea. They discovered a tributary of the Euphrates, an ancient Roman legionary outpost, great bridges, abandoned aqueducts. Vincent identified a Kurdish village as the birthplace of the Greek satirist Lucian. In the mountains of Armenia, on the banks of the Kara Budak, he found an inscription which suggested that the Romans had called these waters by the name they also gave to the river that flowed past Forthampton Court: Sabrina, the Severn. Philology was a hobby of Vincent's. In later life, he zealously searched Joseph Wright's *English Dialect Dictionary* for unfamiliar words he had heard spoken in Gloucestershire. This is among the few things Henry tells us about his father in *Pack My Bag* and the only one that he records with much affection, though to outsiders their relationship seemed by the formal standards of the time relaxed enough.[35] Henry's brother Gerald much later acknowledged that Vincent was more "a *pasha* type of father" than the beating variety.[36] True, he expected his sons to "do things that he liked doing but we didn't like doing," though the example that Gerald recalled was billiards, which Henry at least enjoyed and became good at. Forthampton had a state-of-the-art billiard room designed by Philip Webb, where almost as much ingenuity was needed to adjust a complex series of sliding shutters for the correct light as to pocket the balls. "My father played to win," Henry later said, but "I got good enough to beat him."[37]

Most people who knew him agree that at home the donnish, slightly bullying Vincent lacked charm—certainly by contrast with Maud.[38] Gerald's not-at-all-timid wife, Angela, was to say, "You could never get at him. He was so impersonal. You couldn't communicate at all." Earlier, when Anthony Powell was taken to Forthampton by Henry, he found Vincent "an odd mixture of reserve and rather crude teasing" and added that these were characteristics that Henry inherited.[39] Henry did not, on the other hand, share his father's passion for the classics. He later observed ruefully that while by the age of seven Vincent, like John Reginald before him, was reading Homer in the original, he himself had only just got through the seafaring adventures of Captain Marryat.[40]

If Vincent had married someone else, he might have continued with his existence as part-don, part-explorer, but for the husband of a Wyndham more seemed necessary. So the enterprising John Reginald Yorke helped to secure some directorships for his son and bought him into a failing coppersmith's in Holborn called Pontifex, which had once made plates for William Blake. In a well-planned commercial move that would now be called asset-stripping, Vincent in due course sold the Holborn premises to the *Evening Standard,* moved the factory and many of its workers to a cheaper site in Birmingham (within easy reach of Forthampton), and transferred the Blake engravings to a head office of more manageable size on George Street, W1, behind the Wallace Collection. Under Vincent's energetic, unexpectedly pragmatic chairmanship, Pontifex soon developed unglamorous but very profitable lines in the manufacture of brewery equipment and of plumbing for bathrooms and lavatories. When in London, Vincent and Maud lived in a large Regency terraced house on Mansfield Street, between Harley Street and Portland Place—a short walk from the George Street office. For the rest of his long life, Vincent busily divided his time among London boardrooms, the Birmingham factory, and his Gloucestershire estate.

The elder boys, Philip and Gerald, followed Vincent in being academically clever and outstanding both at team games and at field sports such as hunting and shooting. Henry, by contrast, was plump, uncompetitive, and nervous. He developed as solitary a way of life as he was allowed, spending a lot of his time fishing. An early sense of inadequacy made him identify with anyone else who had little power. While he leaves his ancestors out of *Pack My Bag,* he writes beautifully in it about servants and other local people among whom he grew up. In those first two decades of the century, when the house had no municipal water, gas, or electricity and therefore very few machines except a generator, Forthampton gave employment to a small army of farmworkers, gardeners, grooms, and stable boys. The indoor staff consisted of a butler, two footmen, a hall boy, a cook, a kitchen maid, a scullery maid, five housemaids, and the personal maid of Mrs. Yorke. One of the footmen, named George, much later recalled his life in the household. There is a photograph of George in elaborate livery bearing the family crest—"smothered with the leopard's head," as he put it, "the leopard's head was everywhere." For all this opulence, he remembered his master as having been "a bit on the tight side": When Vincent left a letter in the hall for posting, he first put a stamp on it so that the butler could not fiddle the accounts. "He wasn't chancin' that, for [the butler] to put it down in his book what he thought," George said.[41] This butler was to find his way into Henry's novel *Loving* in the character of Raunce, with his petty financial chicanery.

There were walled gardens on two sides of Forthampton Court, one for roses, which Henry came to love,[42] and a big kitchen garden behind the servants' quarters. To the south and east, the house is surrounded by wide gravel terraces and lawns stretching between flower beds, yew hedges, and shrubberies to the often-flooded river meadows beyond the old moat. Tewkesbury's squat medieval abbey dominates the flat middle ground to the east. One of the fields immediately beyond the garden is called Pigeonhouse Field, and pigeons once flew everywhere in and out of the great trees (in *Blindness*, John Haye persuades his mother to turn the garden into a sanctuary for them). A long drive makes a dogleg into the road leading uphill to the sprawl of timbered redbrick and black-and-white houses that is Forthampton. In Henry's day, the whole village belonged to the Yorkes. It was a self-contained place with a school, a post office, grocery, bakery, blacksmith, wheelwright, men's club, and pub.[43] Even today, when motorways have turned much of the valley on the far side of the Severn between Tewkesbury and Cheltenham into an industrial estate, the undulating lanes around Forthampton lead nowhere and are empty of traffic. To the northwest, along the old Ledbury and Hereford road, the river valley gives way to the hillier country of Malvern Chase. Henry walked and cycled all around here, noticing the place-names with simple relish: Sarn Hill, Volter's, Downend, Agborough, Bishop's Walk, Nabletts Lane, Long Green.[44]

More apprehensively, he rode to hounds. Fox hunting and horse racing were dominant elements of a way of life that, in the infancy of the gasoline-powered engine, was still largely equestrian; or perhaps it is truer to say that rural conservatism required that equestrianism be preserved as a symbol of resistance to change. One member of this world was to write, "field-sports were considered not so much as pleasure as the fulfilment of some sort of sacred national duty."[45] By contrast with his brothers, cousins, and most of his neighbors, Henry was a timid rider, easily embarrassed if his horse misbehaved, but he enjoyed the way in which children out hunting or shooting were suddenly treated as part of the adult world. There was no question, yet, of his not taking part in the normal pursuits of upper-class country life, in which the only element that seemed unusual was Vincent's involvement in Pontifex. From Tuesday to Thursday, Henry's father worked at his London offices and paid regular visits to the smoky, raucous Birmingham works in Tyseley, beside the Grand Union Canal. On Thursday night, he returned to Forthampton, to his horses, hounds, and bulldog, Cerberus,[46] and resumed the life of a country gentleman: rural feudalism underpinned by industrial entrepreneurism—a pattern more common than its practitioners often cared to admit.[47] During the London "season" between March and the end of the Goodwood Races early in August, the whole family moved to town, but even then they spent weekends at Forthampton as often as they could. Vincent ran his estate conscientiously and bought more land when it became available. He was a magistrate. He was an officer in the Royal Gloucestershire Hussars (the local territorial army). He shot and fished. And he rode with the Ledbury Hunt, eventually becoming its Master. The family photograph albums convey something of the gregariousness and ritual of this existence. They are filled with house parties: an alphabet of mansions—Arundel, Burleigh, Cirencester Park—rectangular limousines with the spare wheel above the running board, men with bushy mustaches and sleeked-down hair, women in long gloves and even longer strings of pearls. King George V and Queen Mary appear in these pictures (Vincent's sister Dorothy was one of the queen's ladies-in-waiting),[48] flanked by strong-faced lords, and ladies covered in feathers. They are all off to the races or to a hunt ball.

After Vincent's death in 1957, one of his obituarists recorded cautiously, "His two lives seemed to suit him extremely well, and although it was not easy to tell (for he was very reserved), he was probably a very happy man."[49] Duty may have had as large a part to play in his life as happiness, but perhaps Vincent did not distinguish between the two. Certainly the Yorkes were conscientious landlords. John Reginald had increased the size of the estate at a time of agricultural depression[50] and built a solid village hall as well as the new almshouses: philanthropic constructions that stood in benign contrast to the grim stocks and whipping post by the gate of the medieval church. His daughter-in-law Maud was a devout Anglican, endlessly concerned by and interested in everyone around her. The religious and social conscience of the landed class at this time—what one of their contemporaries, writing about his own mother, called "the spirit of simple virtues and conventional ideals"[51]— is an easy target for satire, and *Blindness* gently mocks Maud's sense of responsibility for the village, the Nursing Association, and the Mother's Union. But this was before the welfare state, and if the squire's wife had not cared, no one else would have. In 1914, though, larger duties were required of the family. Henry Yorke was not yet nine at the beginning of the First World War. As with much in his life, its effects on him were powerful but oblique. At first, no one expected the fighting to go on for long, and Henry's closest relations were either too old or too young to enlist: Vincent was in his mid-forties; Philip and Gerald in their early teens, both at Eton. Still, there were strong military connections in the family. Uncles on both sides of the family were soldiers. Maud's brother-in-law Ivor Maxse, husband of her elder sister Mary, was a regular officer in the Coldstream Guards and a much-decorated veteran of the Sudan and South African wars. When war began, he was promoted to major general. He was to command the Eighteenth Division at the Somme and the Eighteenth Army Corps in Flanders and at Saint Quentin. Vincent's younger brother Ralph was in the Hussars and ended his military career as a brigadier general. All of Maud's five brothers alive in 1914 served in the army, and within months of the outbreak of war one of them, Reginald Wyndham, a captain in the First Life Guards, was killed.[52]

As events dragged on, Vincent and Maud, like a number of other owners of big houses, turned parts of Forthampton Court into a convalescent home for officers suffering from stress—a domestic version of Craiglockhart, the Edinburgh psychiatric hospital where Wilfred Owen met Siegfried Sassoon.[53] At Forthampton, the gassed, the shell-shocked, and the simply terrified sought to calm themselves by riding, fishing, and playing billiards. Twenty or so convalescents could be accommodated in the house at a time. Most were soldiers, but a few were pilots. Henry was enthralled by them all, not least because the stories they told and that were told about them were soon complicated by kinds of behavior for which he had not been prepared by the heroic war lore of the Edwardian upper-class nursery and prep school. To Henry's intense fascination, some had affairs with the maids. One audacious man went shooting out of season, taking "my father's gun, his cartridges and his dog . . . without asking. I remember what upset us as much was the behaviour of my father's dog, that it should lend itself to such practices."[54] But the person who stayed most vividly in the boy's mind was a trembling wretch who had been gassed, could neither eat nor sleep, and screamed at the sound of laughter or the banging of doors. According to *Pack My Bag,* he committed suicide soon after leaving Forthampton. Henry could not forget one episode when the man had seemed better and had set off from the house on a bicycle trip but turned back, wobbling desperately yet evidently determined that the boy not see him fall.[55] To a child, few sights could have brought home an adult's frailty more painfully than an inability to stay on a bike, and the noisy Henry suffered at the thought that it was somehow his fault. His daily encounters with human vulnerability in this period were to mark all of his fiction, most obviously *Back,* about a nerve-shattered veteran of Henry's own world war, which was to come twenty-five years later. There are characters throughout his work who are made to feel more than they can manage.

In some cases, his characters' emotions also seem incommensurate with what prompts them. Such incongruities were to intrigue Henry Green. He believed that they were more common than not—that appropriateness was perhaps the true oddity. This perception was complicated by an upbringing that made him at some levels profoundly conventional. The image of unfitness with which *Pack My Bag* begins—the mouth-breather with a silver spoon—is related immediately to a guilty sense of historical displacement: "I was born . . . three years after one war [the South African War] and nine before another, too late for both." The book obsessively recalls comic minor gaffes, especially ill-timed laughter—occasions when social propriety was overthrown by what he romantically called the "wild delight . . . like sunlight" that came over him both as a child and later. He had an extremely loud laugh.

One spur to such reflections was his inability, as he perceived it, to show the correct responses when, in 1917, his brother Philip died of lymphatic leukemia. If illness had not killed Philip, of course, the last years of the war might well have, but either way he was dead and Henry wasn't, and the parents never fully got over their loss. Their reactions left Henry feeling more inadequate than ever. Vincent and Maud had grown up in Queen Victoria's reign, and their grief was superlative. For forty years, Philip's bedroom on the first floor of Forthampton Court was kept as a shrine. He was a star at Eton when he died, having won a scholarship to the school and distinguished himself at games. His mother preserved his bedroom display of sporting caps, team lists, and other athletic paraphernalia and solemnly brought home the furniture from his room at school—the traditional ottoman and bureau and a table with flaps, which had *Yorke* carved deeply into it. These were joined by Philip's ashes in a Grecian urn, specially commissioned from Omar Ramsden, a leading silversmith of the period. As time passed, Maud eventually allowed Philip's bedroom to be occupied by her maid, Mabel. But all around Mabel, Philip's relics remained, to be displaced only when his brother Gerald took over Forthampton after Vincent's death in 1957.

In an old family house, the dead mix easily with the living, but by any standard these commemorations were exceptionally intense. Henry recoiled from the weight of expectation that had been attached to Philip and which now extended to himself. There was to be no escape from it, even at school.

IN THE YEARS PRIOR TO PHILIP'S DEATH, AFTER AN inconspicuous spell at a private day school that his brothers had also attended in Portman Square, close to the Yorkes' London house,[56] Henry was sent to the promotionally named New Beacon, a prep school in Sevenoaks, Kent. Philip had preceded him there. (Gerald went to Sunningdale.) In the ground-floor School Room, where the boys kept their books in doorless lockers like large pigeonholes, the walls were hung with team photographs and honors boards listing former pupils who had distinguished themselves academically. In 1913, Philip Yorke had won the school's best-ever scholarship to Eton, so there, in gold paint, was—and still is—his name.

War had not yet begun. Henry's account of his early schooldays in *Pack My Bag*, written just before the Second World War, is overcast by later events and by Wordsworthian ideas about fallings-off from childhood freshness. There is also a sense, common to many romantic autobiographies (especially literary ones), that the author must mark himself as unusually wounded. Green was too honest to be unaware of false nuances in the book and often throws off his lugubriousness by describing the kind of unspecific childhood happiness that, as he says, is so hard to recall: "We . . . were extraordinarily gay. We laughed, we screamed and shouted and went about in packs. . . . But all this, apart from a general feeling I have that I was very happy there, all this has gone."[57] Although he does not say so, he himself prompted some of the laughter and gaiety around him. He was, recalled Anthony Powell, "an unremitting talker . . . hit or miss in content, but, as often as not, funny, perceptive, entirely individual." One of his reports in 1917 commented on his "great success in a comic part in the school theatricals."[58]

Powell arrived at New Beacon when he and Henry Yorke were almost eleven. They were to become close friends, following superficially similar paths through prep school, Eton, Oxford, and the social and literary worlds of the 1920s. The novels they were to write have little in common (although there are resemblances between *Party Going* and Powell's *Afternoon Men,* as well as some of the more phantasmagoric episodes in *A Dance to the Music of Time*). But at school the future authors developed in tandem, starting as dormitory storytellers in the half hour after lights-out when talking was still permitted. Their stories, Powell remembers, were usually "re-hashes of popular novels, or serials running in magazines; in neither case works specifically intended for boys, though no doubt tending to possess a detective or thriller basis."[59] They didn't write them down but at one stage briefly began a novel together, sitting on the radiators of the gym. Powell remembers his friend as having been "always interested in words, repeating unfamiliar ones (e.g. hirsute) over to himself, laughing at them, discussing them." During a holiday at Forthampton, they pored over two volumes of Rabelais that they found in the library ("The name even then conveyed unspeakable obscenities").[60]

Powell's father, like the fathers of many boys at the school, was a professional soldier. War was in the air: literally so when the curve of hills to the north of Sevenoaks began to catch the sound of gunfire from across the Channel. It was a small school, seventy-five boys in all, but thirty-seven former pupils and two masters were killed between 1914 and 1918. One of the old boys who died was a twenty-eight-year-old engineer named Hamo Sassoon, hit by a sniper's bullet at Gallipoli and commemorated in a poem by his younger brother Siegfried, also an Old Beaconian.[61] As the months passed, everyone knew someone who died or whose father died, and it became common to see a boy wandering around the edge of the playing field in the respectful purdah to which the bereaved were miserably consigned. An atmosphere of excited mysticism developed, heightened by what Powell describes as "frequent and remorseless promptings that the men in the trenches"—who included the headmaster's two sons, as well as some of his colleagues—"were having a worse time than ourselves," and also by communal singing of "The School at War," a patriotic hymn written by an Eton housemaster:

> *We don't forget you in this dark December.*
> *We sit in schoolrooms that you know so well;*
> *And hear the sounds that you so well remember,*
> *The clock, the hurrying feet, the chapel bell. . . .*
> *We don't forget you in the wint'ry weather*
> *You man the trench, or tramp the frozen snow.*
> *We play the games we used to play together,*
> *In days of peace—that seem so long ago.*

After a succession of late nights spent watching the first air raids, Henry and some others eventually convinced themselves that they had seen a home-guard contingent of the "Angels of Mons"—ghostly visions reported by many soldiers at the front—stalking the school grounds. More tangible evidences of war were the pieces of shrapnel that rattled on the roof and were retrieved eagerly the next morning, to be hidden in the dormitories. Henry's uncle, General Maxse, found time to send him some old maps of the trenches around Passchendaele, but the headmaster, presumably fearful of a breach of security, confiscated them.[62]

The boys were taken to London to see the defenses that had been prepared there in case of invasion. They were also put to war work, knitting khaki scarves and—with the scarcity of both food and labor—growing vegetables in the gardens. Pigs, too, were kept (a detail that, thirty years on, was to find its way into the futuristic girls' school in Henry Green's novel *Concluding*).[63] But for the most part, school was still school. The curriculum, like the building, was late Victorian, the main elements mathematics, Latin, French, and English grammar, with occasional periods of art and music. Then there was gym, which Henry detested, and other semirecreational pursuits such as carpentry, in the course of which he produced a pipe rack for his father and three rickety tables destined for the bedsides of the convalescents at Forthampton. He best liked activities that most resembled those of home: keeping caterpillars in a box in a garden shed, watching homing pigeons, splashing about in the pool, or going for long walks in the high-hedged sunken lanes around Sevenoaks. On Sundays, dressed in their best suits and wide, stiff collars, the boys were often taken into the deer park of Knole, the Elizabethan mansion of the Sackville-Wests, on the edge of the town. With a characteristic mixture of neoromanticism and bathos, Henry says in *Pack My Bag* that it was there that he "began to have those first movements of delight, those first motions toward the open heart which is growing up . . . looking beauty right in her cow eyes."[64]

New Beacon's headmaster and owner was John Stewart Norman, who had taken over the school in 1863 and brought it to its present site in 1900. Until the war, his sons also taught there, one of them returning as its next headmaster, and the snobbish Norman took pride in building up similar family continuities among the boys. A recent ex-pupil was Viscount Weymouth, son of the marquess of Bath and heir to Longleat. He was killed in the war, and his younger brother, who took his title, followed him to the school shortly after Henry Yorke. One of the things *Pack My Bag* describes first about New Beacon is Norman's announcement that a lord was about to arrive. It was the first time Henry had noticed the existence of snobbery.[65]

Prep schools and their masters are the subject of a minor comic subgenre of English literature. In *Infants of the Spring,* the first volume of his autobiography, Anthony Powell is careful to distance himself from contemporary practitioners such as George Orwell, Cyril Connolly, Evelyn Waugh, and John Betjeman,[66] but even so, he falls into some of their routines, and it is interesting to compare his description of Norman with Henry Green's more unusual version in *Pack My Bag*. To both writers, the head inevitably had his grotesque side. Green calls him a tyrant, a monster, a "remarkable old man of a violent appearance." Powell describes him as looking like Kipling, with "sparse grey hair, drooping tobacco-stained moustache, abnormally thick spectacles, eternal old thick tweed suit, worn whatever the climate." For Powell, though, such routinely observed eccentricities are as far as his interest takes him. Green, by contrast, while finding Norman no less bizarre, also searches out what made him more substantial—a figure whom the young Henry feared and mocked but also admired, even loved. This in turn involves remembering what it was like to be a boy in not only its comic and romantic elements but also its gauche ones.

Among the aspects of childhood recorded by Green but often left out by comparable autobiographers is intense religiosity. Perhaps with Joyce's *Portrait of the Artist* in mind, he quotes at length from a muddled, deeply sanctimonious sermon written when he was about twelve.[67] Then there is hero worship, along with the underlying conformism that Powell came to see as a crucial element in Henry's divided character. He puzzled not so much over what the school rules were as over which you should break if you wanted to be popular.[68] And he worried about conflicts between authentic feeling and social orthodoxy, particularly in the contrast between the headmaster's instant tears over Philip Yorke's death—"He took off his spectacles and became helpless"—and his own guilt-inducing unresponsiveness. The value that Henry put on "that instinct for privacy boys have who dream" may have been reinforced by the beginnings of deafness—while at the school, he suffered from mastoiditis[69]—as well as by the crushing codes of English schoolboys: "prisoners from ourselves," as he later described them, obliged to hide even their own parents' letters, "those secrets of tenderness." Norman, whom he respected and wanted to please, half convinced him that any secret was a guilty one.[70] The dilemma was made even more difficult by Henry's innocence. He was physically shy, knew next to nothing about girls, and seems to have been completely ignorant of such homosexual relations as went on in the school.[71] It was in these indirect ways that New Beacon nurtured the imagination of a secretive boy with little to hide except a belief that you should tell the truth.

Artists often see truth at an oblique angle, but while truthfulness was one of Green's values, intensity was another. To his friends, it was clear that he often exaggerated, whether for comic or poetic effect: not a remarkable characteristic in itself, but one that made him enigmatic because of the contrast with his objectivity at other times. Anthony Powell was particularly struck by how the mixture affected Henry's sense of his relations with his mother and father. He talked as if he was precociously detached from them, startling Powell by announcing, when he was about eleven, "The fact is that both my parents are extremely selfish." But when Powell first stayed at Forthampton, he was surprised by how cheerfully the family got along. Vincent and Maud seemed fond of and amused by Henry, whose nickname was "Goosy," and Henry ragged Vincent in a way that Powell, who had been led to expect a relationship at least as formal as the one he had with his own father, found almost shocking. In Henry's early writing, his parents and other relations are a source of closely observed comedy that combines ironic detachment with deep affection. One sketch, "Olein," not published in his lifetime, has Maud and Vincent—whom Maud alternately calls "Billy" and by his middle name, Wodehouse—vigorously discussing various domestic matters, starting with whether their guest, Maud's cousin Olein Wyndham-Quinn, over on a visit from Ireland, should or should not be encouraged to eat an apple before her soup ("Oh no Vincent I can't allow this. It is like savages and their pig tub").[72] In all this, various questions are addressed to Olein, among them whether she spoils her nephews and nieces in the way the couple claim they both spoil Henry, without her ever being given a chance to answer. The impression of a warm, companionable marriage confirms Powell's recollection.

HENRY BELIEVED THAT, BECAUSE OF THE PRECEDENT set by Philip, his headmaster as well as his parents expected him to succeed academically. It was to this, rather than to any merit of his own, that he attributed "the rare summer of [Norman's] smile."[73] (When Norman showed him off to potential parents, on the other hand, the boy assumed that it was because he was fat and would be taken as an advertisement for the school's food.)[74] Here was one of the many disappointments for which he allowed himself to feel responsible. With his background, he was unlikely to have been turned away by Eton in those days, but when the time came to take the exam, he did not do well. He knew, too, that when he got to the school he would be compared there not only with the dead Philip and with their prizewinning, games-playing father, but with the robustly alive Gerald. Gerald Yorke was on the cricket team, was head of his house, and was a member of the elite club known self-explanatorily as Pop. At Eton, *Yorke* was quite a name.

CHAPTER 2

Society of Arts

THE ADULT CHARACTERS IN HENRY GREEN'S NOVELS did not go to school. With a handful of exceptions, they have had no childhoods, no formative early experiences; they exist in a perpetual amnesia—comic or dejected or intense but always seemingly unconscious of most of what went before. Schools figure in the stories only if they are part of the present. *Blindness* begins at a version of Eton. *Concluding* is set in a futuristic training college for girls who are going to be state functionaries. In Green's last novel, *Doting,* a callow boy named Peter returns home from school during the holidays, to the disruption of his parents' routines. But there is no equivalent in these books of Anthony Powell's emphasis on formation and development and on the comic correspondences or incongruities between people's careers at school and later. Powell's *A Dance to the Music of Time* consoles readers by saying both that the people who don't succeed in life are often the most interesting (such as the reckless Stringham) and that success can come to the least likely people (such as Widmerpool—a figure of fun at Eton). Powell's worldview is completely Etonian: life as essentially a continuation of school. To Green, almost everything is now.

In 1918, however, *now* meant Eton. At no other school have the pupils been more aware of their place in a closed, privileged community—one whose alumni at that time still had a dominant role in the running of Great Britain and, through its colonies, of a sizable portion of the globe. From the point of view of the typical new boy, his contemporaries fell into at least one of two main categories: those who were related to him or to friends of his family, and those who had names that appeared every day in the newspapers. In addition to Henry's brother, Gerald, his cousins Rupert Biddulph and John and Frederick Maxse (the general's sons) were also at the school. The Biddulphs lived near the Yorkes, at Ledbury Park, Herefordshire. Other neighbors included the earl of Beauchamp, whose country home was Madresfield Court, Malvern, and two of whose sons, Viscount Elmley and Hugh Lygon, were also among Henry's school contemporaries. In the second category, there was Arthur Baldwin, whose father would become prime minister, and John Mosley, whose elder brother was to lead the British Union of Fascists; there were boys named Baring, Guinness, Hambro, Harmsworth, Pakenham, and Sackville-West; there was Prince Leopold of Belgium and Prince Nicholas of Romania, and Prince Sarabjit Singh of Kapurthala.[1] Among them, as everyone knew, were prospective heads of state, government ministers, colonial administrators, diplomats, chiefs of the armed forces, bankers, and company directors, as well as those destined simply to be the custodians of inherited wealth. Their future pleasures would include drawing on memories such as those of Quintin Hogg, later Lord Hailsham, who as lord chancellor was to reminisce fondly that he "was quite good at the wall game . . . and on one occasion was bitten on the leg by the present Duke of Montrose."[2] Henry himself was caned by a future prime minister, Alec Douglas-Home, who was in the same house.[3]

Success at Eton often appeared to be the most perfect kind of success there could be.[4] Failure, on the other hand, could prompt a correspondingly vivid sympathy with the human lots of which most Etonians had little direct experience. The frustration of Henry's contemporary Frank Pakenham (later Lord Longford, as well as Anthony Powell's brother-in-law) at not being elected to Pop was generally assumed among his school contemporaries to have spurred his subsequent career as a Labour politician and increasingly quixotic social reformer.[5] Henry Green's novels may have been influenced by similar exclusions. Certainly, one of the most obvious differences between his early work and that of Anthony Powell is its strong sympathy for the working class. In this respect it resembles that of George Orwell, a contemporary who, as Eric Blair, passed through the school almost unnoticed.

Henry himself made something of a mark, although at first mainly

by association with Gerald. By the time Yorke the younger arrived at
Eton in the autumn of 1918, while not conspicuously attractive or good
at anything, he wasn't the opposite. He was less plump, and was growing
tall. He joined unskillfully in the school's idiosyncratic team games. He
learned its arcane vocabulary and its elaborate regulations: which side of
the street you were allowed to walk on; which of the intricately varied
and antiquated items of uniform denoted what; who was and who was
not allowed to put his arm through someone else's. And he developed at
least some of the strategies of evasion necessary for survival in what he
later called "a humane concentration camp."[6] As a tentative second violin in the school orchestra, for example, he soon found it better to mime
than to produce wrong notes, claiming later that as a result he had managed to stay unnoticed in the orchestra from his first term at Eton to his
last.

He always derived a wry pleasure from telling self-deprecating stories. Some were exaggerated. His violin playing was competent enough
for him to win an interhouse competition, with the younger, very tal-
ented Alan Pryce-Jones at the piano, though according to Pryce-Jones
Henry's practicing "was agony—the house used to *shake* with bad
notes."[7] More important than whether Henry's modesty was excessive is
what elicited it. In *Pack My Bag,* he points out that he never got onto any
teams at school, was not elected to Pop, and, when the soon-to-be-
famous Eton Society of Arts was first formed, became its secretary ("appropriately enough"), nothing more important.[8] This note of defeatism
may have had something to do with the contrasts between him and his
brothers, but he was a canny autobiographer, and much of what he describes is there to explain, however obliquely, the formation of the writer
Henry Green. A part-calculated subservience gave him scope to observe
not only other people in this self-consciously microcosmic society but
also himself and his feelings.

The strongest of these, at least as he later recalled, was shame. The
amorality of childhood—lies, thefts, betrayal of friends—made him miserable because he had none of the anesthesia that came with social success. When people behaved badly toward him, he knew he was no better.
His emotional life took place on a spectrum between embarrassment and
guilt (described by one of his more louche friends as "life's gift to those
who are selfish, know it, and hate it").[9] As a child, Henry had written a

sermon about Peter, the disciple who when pressed pretended that he did not know Jesus. He was also fascinated by the story of Judas—"I believe it haunts all little boys," he claimed.[10] Sometimes it seemed as though he was chased by such feelings in an emotional fox hunt where quarry and pursuer were indistinguishable. The huntsman, he says plangently in *Pack My Bag,* "blows his horn gently, and the note . . . is shame remembered, a run across familiar country."[11]

If he was guilt-ridden, though, he was also still a lively, talkative, entertaining boy who had two particular sources of happiness in his early months at Eton. One was the armistice, which lifted from him and all his contemporaries—especially the seventeen-year-old Gerald—the doom that had faced them for four years: that they might have to go to France and be killed.[12] (Vincent made the boys celebrate the outcome by spitting on the German embassy in Amsterdam when they were there on holiday, visiting their Dutch relations.)[13] The other was the friendship unexpectedly shown him by his brother.

Gerald was sensitive and extremely intelligent. He missed Philip and had a fair idea of what Henry might face in the competitive, games-oriented, and conformist environment of their school. While direct physical bullying was rare in A. W. Whitworth's well-run if gloomy house, there were many substitutes, of which vandalism was among the most common.[14] Every boy at Eton lives in his own room. Henry's, typically, had a small fireplace and was furnished with a bed, an ottoman, and a small desk with built-in drawers and bookshelves. Pictures carefully chosen for their unobjectionableness—sporting prints and watercolors of the school buildings—hung against the rose-patterned wallpaper. One way to hurt someone was to take these surroundings apart. When Henry was sixteen, he wrote a description of such an episode, and five years later the sketch still mattered enough to him to have seemed worth copying out and showing to a friend at Oxford.[15] The main character, Brown, is sitting in his room when three boys who are described as his friends arrive noisily, throw a chair and, ignoring his mild protests, set about smashing pictures, spilling ink, and scrawling insults on the wall. Henry later wrote that he would never forget his feelings when he heard people running down the corridor outside while he waited like a trapped animal, wondering if it was him they were coming for.[16]

He suffered little until Gerald left for Cambridge in 1920, at the late age of nineteen. Closeness between brothers was not encouraged at Eton, but Gerald would take the younger boy's arm and—another privilege reserved for members of Pop, of which he was now president—lead him across to the sunny side of the town's main street. He gave him tea and let him sit in his room and read. In Henry's books, a halo is written around some people, usually girls, as if he is translating an early Garbo film into prose. Gerald is one of the people romanticized in this way: "As we went forward in the dust . . . windows caught the sun and boys, running through low doorways out of shops, were for the instant blinded before they saw. They would go on laughing until that other brightness of his clothes eclipsed them into . . . silence."[17]

Many boys were jealous of the relationship, and after Gerald had gone to Cambridge, the fifteen-year-old Henry was punished for it. Until then, he both basked in it and took the opportunity it gave him to watch other members of the Eton athletocracy with a closeness that did not exclude irony. "They had no private lives," he was to write, "they had no views, they must be happy. They were there to make runs."[18] For those who were not in the running, whether at sport, socially, or academically, days at Eton were not full. One of the school's distinguishing features was that it left boys a fair amount to their own devices. Lessons started early—there was a class before breakfast. But afternoons were for the most part free except for games, which were compulsory only three days a week. Henry often found himself lonely and with little to do—isolated by, among other things, his relative imperviousness to homosexual attraction. Alan Pryce-Jones's recollection was that Henry was "a rather friendless person, always on his own. He wasn't really interested by . . . um . . . the other boys. There were one or two quite nice ones in the house. Henry didn't respond, I think, to adolescent high spirits."[19] He would mooch around the backs of the fives courts in jealous agony while, four by four, the other boys jumped about and shouted.[20] He was noisy himself and needed an audience, but no one seemed to notice him. He became paranoid—was he being spurned because he had no title, not even an "Honourable"? He began to try too hard. At the annual cadet-force summer camp, a clergyman called for volunteers to tell jokes. Henry stepped forward eagerly but was the only boy to do so and was met with stony silence.[21]

In order to avoid team games, he took up beagling, which reminded him of home and, like other kinds of cross-country running, left the participants essentially to themselves. But now his solitude ended. Through beagling he got to know Robert Byron, a highly intelligent, ambitious, witty, and volatile boy of his own age who had spent a peripatetic childhood and won a scholarship to Eton. His parents now lived in Savernake Forest, in Wiltshire. Byron found school boring and stuffy. He hated conventions of any kind, including politeness. (Asked what he would like best in the world, he answered, "To be an incredibly beautiful male prostitute with a sharp sting in my bottom.") He was amused and impressed by Henry: "He can talk like no other person I've ever met," Byron wrote to his mother in February 1922. "He is also very funny."[22] And Henry, through his family, seemed to know "everyone with a mind in England." The liking was reciprocated, and Robert and Henry competed to invite each other home, Henry preparing Robert for his first visit by caricaturing his parents, as he had done with Anthony Powell. Vincent Yorke was "just like a large negro—he will shake you by the hand and run away— my mother will quarrel with you at once and then be charming—do come." So Byron went to stay with the Yorkes at their London house over the Easter holidays, reporting amusedly to his mother about the size of their car: "We were met at Paddington by a palace that drove us to the house."[23] They went to the cinema every day, partly to escape from what seemed to them the tiresome repartee between Vincent and Gerald ("Sarcasm flew"). One evening, there was a family outing to the theater to see Mary Roberts Rhinehart and Avery Hopwood's popular mystery, *The Bat*—a resplendent social occasion, "Mrs Yorke in a striped gold and black very long and tight-fitting gown. . . . The King and Queen [George V and Queen Mary] were in a box. . . . Lady Dalhousie was opposite them, her neck and bosom literally blazing with diamonds." The next day, they were taken to the zoo and to a concert before Vincent went off to Gloucestershire for a diocesan conference and Henry finally extricated himself and Robert for another trip to the cinema, where they ate a box of chocolates instead of having tea.[24]

Byron's interest in the visual arts made him, for his age, an unusual guest. He admired the Yorkes' Adam house and its Angelica Kauffmann ceilings, and had long conversations with Maud about Petworth and her brother's unpopular reluctance to let members of the public see its art collection. Back at Eton, this eager, un-English–seeming level of sophistication also ingratiated him with Harold Acton, Brian Howard, and others in a small group of like-minded rebels who called themselves "aesthetes," partly by contrast with athletes but mainly to assert their belief in the values of art—especially (though to different degrees) in the art of modernism. They were dandyish in a way that descended directly from the 1890s, as well as from the older tradition of Beau Brummell. The image of the more camp among them has been fixed by the beautiful, whimsical, self-destructive Brian Howard, especially in how he was fictionalized in Evelyn Waugh's *Brideshead Revisited*. It was Howard who hired a room at the back of a jeweler's in Eton where he and Acton played Russian ballet music on a gramophone and danced together, impersonating Massine and Nijinsky.[25] It was also Howard who punningly pretended a fascination with campanology, stressing the first syllable and urging that every house in the school build its own belfry so that "it could be distinguished both musically and architecturally" (he wondered whether the bells could be bought at Cartier's).[26]

The historian of the Eton aesthetes, Martin Green, calls the group the "children of the sun" and has seen them in mythological terms as acting out an Oedipal rebellion against their squirearchical, militaristic fathers. But he also rightly admits the limitations of this pattern. In the first place, the people involved were of very different types. They included not only dandies such as Oliver Messel and Hugh Lygon but a boy from Henry's house named Colin Anderson, who defied the group's own conventions not only by being good at games but by getting into Pop. And while Martin Green divides his *Sonnenkinder* into three main subgroups—the dandy-aesthete, the rogue, and the naïf—he does not try to categorize Henry Yorke, who was partly all of these and almost equally their opposites. Besides, in terms of breaking away from First World War values, the most rebellious-seeming were in fact those who had least far to go. The fathers of Brian Howard and Harold Acton were not English squires but successful American painters and art dealers, while Hugh Lygon's father, the seventh earl of Beauchamp, was to be hounded out of England because of his homosexuality. And not everyone in the group was at all outrageous. Anthony Powell, whose father was a soldier, far from symbolically murdering him became a sergeant in the school corps and studied military customs and regalia.

Most of Henry Yorke's own forms of rebellion were either conventional or halfhearted. Like many teenage boys, he and his friends drank a good deal and flattered each other on their self-destructiveness: "How long do your people expect you to live at this rate of debauchery?" Robert Byron asked him, later joking that if Henry died, he would become Hallam to Robert's Tennyson.[27] Having grown out of his prepschool religiosity, Henry briefly resisted the more or less automatic process by which schoolboys were prepared for Anglican Confirmation but, when challenged by Maud, explained hastily that he had forgotten and would put the matter right the following year.[28] One decision that on its face seems consistent with Martin Green's interpretation was Henry's resignation, when he was seventeen, from the school's Officer Training Corps. This certainly irritated his housemaster, but there was nothing impulsive or superficially attention-seeking about it. By looking through the corps' charter in the library, Henry and Robert discovered not only that it had been founded in Victorian times and was therefore in terms of the school's history a relatively recent innovation, but that until the First World War membership had been voluntary.[29] Even those who joined had been allowed to resign if they had their parents' support.[30] Vincent and Maud did not oppose Henry, several other boys took the same route, and the school responded with its well-known tolerance. At dinner at the headmaster's house some time later, the conversation turned to the corps' forthcoming trip to the Royal Tournament. Henry joked that he and the other resigners should form "an ex-service man's brigade," which could accompany the main parade. The headmaster's wife offered to organize the knitting of a banner, and a bishop who was among the guests said he would act as chaplain. Henry's housemaster, with whom he never got along,[31] delivered some sour comments at the end of that term (the autumn of 1922). Yorke, he wrote, "has a joie de vivre which only demands a succession of sensations, thrills & shocks to keep him quite happy. . . . He has not a germ of public spirit that I can see."[32] But worse school reports have been known.

The other gestures that he risked at school—wearing an unusually long overcoat, decorating his room with a horse's straw hat on which he had painted concentric red and yellow rings—could be considered outrageous only by the stuffiest of standards. To Anthony Powell, looking back, Henry was "the very reverse of a dashing figure. He was very careful about not being that. He was in a kind of way terrifically conventional."[33] Indeed, most members of the group—Brian Howard and Hugh Lygon excepted—proved to be at root prudent and hardworking, and several became conspicuously productive writers. Of these, some—notably Powell—had longer careers than others, but all made rapid starts. While Brian Howard was still at school he had a poem and a satire published in the magazine *New Age* and a drawing included in the 1920 International Exhibition.[34] Harold Acton's collection *Aquarium* appeared in his second term at Oxford; *Blindness* in Green's second year there. Within a decade of leaving Eton, Acton had published seven books—mainly poetry and history—Robert Byron another seven (travel and art history), Powell was established as a publisher and had brought out three novels, Cyril Connolly and Alan Pryce-Jones were prolific literary journalists, and Alan Clutton-Brock was art critic of *The Times*. Bryan Guinness, who, though not a member of the Society of Arts, was also among Henry's friends (they used to joke that they had a common family interest in brewing), had established himself as a poet and novelist.[35] Henry Green, in the same period, had published *Blindness* and *Living*, had married and settled into the head office of Pontifex, and was at work on two further novels. Not for the first time in English history, men who cultivated a reputation for dilettantism proved unexpectedly ambitious, dedicated, and—if in varying degrees and for different durations—robust.

Several of them sooner or later published memoirs: Pryce-Jones as early as 1936,[36] Connolly in 1938, Green in 1940, Acton in 1948, Powell characteristically both later and more copiously.[37] So readers may have heard a lot about the Eton Society of Arts. For all their gifts, to outsiders its members often looked, and look, like spoiled poseurs. When Harold Acton nostalgically describes his and Brian Howard's Sunday visits to Slough, where they wandered the streets imagining themselves as the Goncourt brothers in search of copy and speculating about the atrocities of witchcraft and fetishism that might be found behind the town's front doors, the reader wonders how they seemed to the churchgoing couples whom they watched with supercilious glee.[38] But every artist's

magistrates, bankers. One of them, Robert, born in 1801, became the member of Parliament for Hereford, as did his elder son, Michael, grandfather of Dig and Mary. A lively, forceful man, Michael Biddulph sat in parliament for thirty-five years and was rewarded with a hereditary peerage in 1903. He became connected to the Yorkes by his second marriage, to a daughter of the earl of Hardwicke, and in 1896 his eldest son, John, added another link by marrying Marjorie Mure, a granddaughter of the first Lord Leconfield. So John Biddulph's children were distant cousins of Gerald and Henry Yorke.

There were four of them. Dig was born in 1901 and registered under the names Mary Adelaide. The second name, which was her grandmother's, was formally abbreviated to Adèle, but as a young child she was slow to speak, and the first word she uttered sounded like "dig," which stuck for the rest of her life.[41] By a Henry-like quirk, her first name was the name by which her younger sister, born in 1906, was actually called, but Mary also had a nickname, "Miss." The girls had two brothers, Michael and Rupert, born in 1898 and 1904. Like Vincent Yorke, John Biddulph wanted his sons to thrive in the family business, but Biddulph's wish was to be frustrated. Michael was of the right age to fight in the First World War. A lieutenant in the Coldstream Guards, he was wounded in the legs and shell-shocked; he never fully recovered, never had a job, and after he inherited Ledbury Park in the harsh economy of 1949, sold it off. Michael's problems may not have been exclusively due to the war. There was a strain of instability in the family; his brother, Rupert, ended his days in an asylum.[42]

These were among the difficulties about which, all their lives, Dig and Mary preferred not talk—perhaps not even to think. So it is hard to tell whether the fact that in different ways they both fell lastingly in love with the eccentric, wayward Henry Yorke was a sign of independence of spirit or of its opposite—an instinctive attraction to a cousin whose fragility in some ways echoed that of their brothers.

HENRY'S OWN BROTHER, MEANWHILE, WAS ABOUT TO fall under the spell of the magician, adventurer, drug addict, and pornographic poet Aleister Crowley. With his creed "Do What Thou Wilt," Crowley—then in his early fifties—had, in the words of his enthusiastic biographer John Symonds, "seized the imagination of the restless world."[43] For most of the restless it was a temporary infatuation, but from the day when Gerald Yorke first wrote to Crowley, he was to become one of the most faithful as well as closest disciples of the man known to readers of *John Bull* as "the Worst Man in Britain," "the King of Depravity," and eventually "the Wickedest Man in the World."[44] To the bewildered fury of his parents, "Brother Volo Intelligere" ("I want to understand") became one of Crowley's financiers and acted as a kind of go-between, explaining and excusing Crowley to Scotland Yard and later annotating manuscripts and proofs of his works, paying to have some of them printed, and meticulously filing the letters that "The Great Beast" received from fascinated contemporaries such as Nancy Cunard, Aldous Huxley, H. L. Mencken, and Bertrand Russell. The collection, somewhat depleted by more recent and less scrupulous admirers, now occupies a smoldering corner of the Warburg Institute, London.

Gerald had gone up to Trinity College, Cambridge—Crowley's old college—in 1920 and took the best degree in history awarded at the university in his year.[45] He stayed at Trinity until the spring of 1924, trying for a Prize Fellowship (in which he was beaten by Steven Runciman, the future historian of the Crusades) and working on a thesis, about spying on the Northwest Frontier, that he did not complete. He then spent a short period in business, first as a trainee accountant, then in the London office of Pontifex, experiences he hated.[46] Part of the problem, which Henry satirized in *Living,* was the conflict between Vincent's determination to bring his brilliant elder son into the family firm and his equally strong reluctance to allow him any space or listen to any of his ideas. But Gerald's incoherent sense of himself in any case had less to do with City boardrooms and industrial contracts than with what he had inherited from the now long-submerged part of his father: the explorer and adventurer. In the 1930s, Gerald went to the Far East, traveled extensively in China, experimented with drugs, took up Yoga and Buddhism, and generally pioneered the routes that many other young Westerners were to follow in later generations.

Around the time of Henry's superficially more modest if essentially no less daring departure for working-class Birmingham, Gerald had begun an affair with Sarah Rummel, wife of the concert pianist Walter Rummel. She had succeeded Isadora Duncan in Rummel's affections and was herself, as Henry wrote to Tony Powell, "a theosophist & a prominent religious dancer. You know, they dance to hymns & get into transports, so dull, but it rouses Gerald's worst passions & makes him even more of a bore than he is already."[47] In their parents' terms, the escapade was catastrophic, and the mood at home became fraught. Henry's feelings were divided. He had no strong views on sexual morality, liked and admired his brother, and in many ways wanted to support him. But Gerald had always stood in Henry's light. At a time when the younger man was especially keen to prove himself, there was an inevitable element of schadenfreude in the situation. He relayed the story to friends with excited horror, pleading both for secrecy and for any gossip they might have. Was the woman promiscuous? How would Rummel react? If the affair ended in court, Henry not unoptimistically speculated, the damages might be enormous. "A divorce would nearly kill my family and the money side would leave them homicidal."[48]

Gerald was suffering a breakdown, described in the family alternately as neurasthenia and as religious mania. To Vincent and Maud, as to the Biddulph parents, psychological collapse was always due to lack of moral fiber, though Henry worked hard to persuade his mother that blaming Gerald for his condition was like "blaming the car for having no petrol" (which in fact she might equally well have done). The true cause, he argued—perhaps partly for reasons of his own—was "home life," from which Gerald wanted to escape. His parents' anger would only make things worse.[49] Henry said that he would put the same view in person to Vincent, though a few months later, when his brother was trying to help Crowley to get a book of memoirs published, Henry told their father that Gerald was as "daft as a hatter."[50]

In the spring of 1928, partly to get Gerald away from Sarah Rummel, Vincent took him and Henry on a business trip via New York and New Orleans to Mexico. Henry was always unenthusiastic about travel ("It interferes with my masturbation," he told Anthony Powell)[51] and never shook off the assumption, more common than not among the English, that foreigners were intrinsically risible. From New York, he wrote to his mother about how odd, especially how confessional, he found Americans, although he pretended to deplore his father's habit of exclaiming in their hearing, "Dreadful people, dreadful, I do hate them so."[52] Every man in New York was middle-aged, it seemed to Henry, and every other man Jewish.[53] As for women, in New York they were less sensual than those in New Orleans—a distinction not made by Vincent, or so Henry claimed in a description to Powell of a trip to a Broadway music hall, where the sixty-year-old "insisted on leaning over a girl on the row immediately below him & staring at her dugs."[54] Henry's own encounters with American girls occurred largely in wealthy houses, where they told him all about Wellesley and about how many men they knew at Princeton and Harvard; but at least he understood what they were saying. In the heat and dust of Mexico, his ignorance of Spanish reduced people to "floods of tears, wailing & gnashing their teeth." Cooling himself under the revolving fan of his hotel room, he communicated with the staff through a harassed interpreter in the lobby, to whom they all spoke on the telephone, passing the receiver from hand to hand.[55] Robert Byron responded to such tales by criticizing how little his friend valued experience for its own sake. Surely he could have found something to please him, if only the fact that "transatlantic emptiness would have swelled your self-estimation—I always feel twice as important, in fact a tiny magnificent product of evolution, when *I* meet an American."[56]

Henry had little to say to his friends about the Compania Limitada del Ferrocarril Mexicano, into whose mysteries his father, as chairman of the board, hoped to initiate his sons. And the journey was to make hardly any impression on *Living*. The migrating birds that he saw from the ship gave him a metaphor for the daydreams of the working-class heroine, Lily Gates, but otherwise the novel's only echo of his experiences is heard in Dick Dupret's mental dismissal of wanderlust, which Lily represents: "One might go to foreign countries but what was in these but nausea of travelling, hotels, trains, languages you did not know, Americans?"[57]

AFTER HE RETURNED TO ENGLAND, HENRY CONTINued to spend time at Forthampton and on Mansfield Street, both to see Dig—whose parents were not only country neighbors but had a house in Knightsbridge[58]—and to work on his novel.[59] But he felt increasingly ill at ease with the whole tribe of Yorkes, Wyndhams, Maxses, and the rest, who endlessly met to keep abreast of one another's "dingy movements."[60] He would soon be twenty-three and wanted to make his own life: the life of a modern young man in love, and of a writer, and also of someone who had now measured the gap between the assumptions of his parents' world and how most other people lived. Although he resisted ideologies and—despite a widespread reputation to the contrary—never shared the socialist convictions, however short-lived in some cases, of contemporaries such as Graham Greene, Nancy Mitford, Frank Pakenham, and Peter Quennell, he saw what was around him, more as a spectator and recorder than a participant, yet perhaps for that reason more clearly than others did. In August 1928, he commented on the struggles of industry in Birmingham, particularly of local motor manufacturers, who he presciently said would be put out of business by Ford, which had already embarked on a venture in Cowley. High unemployment in the West Midlands was causing a mood of palpable resentment, which he experienced as a challenge as much as a worry: He couldn't understand why Robert Byron—then in Czechoslovakia—had to go abroad to look for excitement.[61]

A few weeks later, some of the men at Pontifex invited him to the local railwaymen's club on condition that he didn't "talk posh." By the end of the evening, as he proudly related to his mother, he had been elected a member.[62] The occasion may have been a party for his departure. Henry had agreed with his parents that once he had completed the new novel, he would move to London and join the managerial side of the business. He was determined, though, that this should not entail living in Mansfield Street; in August 1928 he had sent Maud a long, rather surly letter on the subject. They simply did not have enough in common, he told her. She must "face up to the fact that by nature I am not the sort of person who dresses for dinner every night, in fact I am not what is generally known as a gentleman."[63] He had had enough of "listening every day to dialogues about horses & hounds" and being obliged to respond with monologues of his own about books. The alternative he proposed was that he should live in bachelor lodgings in London, as did Anthony Powell and several other friends. He could then amicably visit Mansfield Street a couple of times a week. He did not mention another possibility, which was suggested by the recent marriage of Evelyn Waugh.[64]

Waugh was the second of Henry's friends to have married since he had gone to Birmingham. The first, even less expectedly, was Nevill

Coghill, whose new ménage was a topic of ardent discussion between Henry and Wystan Auden. Auden's home was in Birmingham, and at Coghill's suggestion he had made contact with Henry there in March 1928.[65] To the young poet, Coghill's having married not only seemed as improbable as it did to many of his close friends but also was a personal challenge. Nevill had previously been "completely homosexual," Wystan wrote to Henry, adding that his wife was "very young—actually my twin." He thought that she had "no measure of detachment from her impulses and reactions." Henry was not troubled by the last consideration, which was equally true of himself, and was as intrigued by the Coghills' comfortable home at Hinksey Hill as he was by the new question of how the Waughs, "he-Evelyn" and "she-Evelyn," would live. In their case, the first signs were not encouraging. After a brief honeymoon near Oxford, the impoverished couple lived apart for three months while Waugh did battle with publishers over *Decline and Fall*. But by September, the book had appeared to good reviews, and Waugh and his wife were busy decorating an apartment that they had found in Islington. It became a popular meeting place for their friends, to some of whom it represented an idyll of innocent, devoted domesticity. Within months, Bryan Guinness, in turn, married the eighteen-year-old Diana Mitford.[66] "The fact is," Henry observed tactlessly to Anthony Powell, "everyone gets married who can afford to."[67]

Henry arranged for the two Evelyns to come and stay at Forthampton, taking some pains in planning the visit,[68] inviting Robert Byron for the same weekend and briefing Maud about she-Evelyn and the friends they had in common, especially Pansy Pakenham—yet another of Henry's acquaintances who married that year.[69] In the event, she-Evelyn fell ill with German measles, and the Waughs didn't come.[70] Whether or not in Henry's mind the plan had been consciously related to thoughts of marriage, the idea came still closer when "Miss" Biddulph became engaged to a good-looking young guards officer, Monty Lowry-Corry. It wasn't long before Henry took Dig to Oxford to meet Nevill Coghill and some of his other friends.[71]

Everyone liked her, and Nevill later told Henry that Maurice Bowra thought her "brilliant."[72] Bowra always exaggerated, and he was also an ironist, so the report is hard to assess, all the more since Dig eluded even the sharpest observers. Tony Powell found her "rather a sleepy character . . . very sweet, not very bright," and others describe her as fey and languishing in a way that might or might not have disguised keen intelligence. "She was very sweet," one confirms. "I don't know about her brain at all."[73] "Dig is *so* nice," Robert Byron wrote simply to his mother, having had dinner with her and Henry. Brilliant or not, it was agreed that she was exceptionally good-natured and beautiful. Henry himself was in no doubt. "She has a stupendous intellect," he assured Evelyn Waugh, "behind an enormous capacity for idleness & an appearance of innocuousness."[74]

WHILE THE RELATIONSHIP WAS DEVELOPING, HENRY finished his novel. Like all his books, *Living* contains a thread of coded autobiography, and much of what he had experienced since leaving Oxford went into it: factory life, of course, but also the tensions between grown-up children and their parents and the confusions of young love affairs. Lily, playing her two admirers off against each other, longing both to break away from her upbringing and to find a familiar kind of domesticity, is almost as much a portrait of the artist as is Dick Dupret. But it is in Dick that Henry Green satirized both himself and his brother.

As a writer of social comedy, Green has never enjoyed the popularity of Evelyn Waugh or Anthony Powell, but his novels, though less interested in indulging the reader's fantasies, are often as funny as theirs, partly because of the quiet hostility with which he conveys his world. Early in *Living,* Dick complains about his "grimy and tiring" first visit to his father's factory.[75] He is dining with his mother, who, having left her handkerchief upstairs, sends the footman in search of it, and then, in search of the footman, the butler, both of whose wages are presumably paid for by all that grime, although it does not seem to be this that leads Dick to concede that the foundry has "a kind of romance about it . . . the castings, they call them, were very moving."[76] By contrast with his friends, however, reflections such as these make him seem a figure of Ruskinian gravitas. His rival for the affections of Hannah Glossop, for example, is a youth whose chief accomplishment is the ability to move from sitting to lying down with a full tumbler of water on his head. "No one could do it after him," the beguilingly deadpan narrative relates, "many got soused with water in trying to do it, which only added to the general hilarity. Hannah got quite hysterical with excitement."[77]

The story does not spare Dick Dupret, always catching him picking his nose behind his engagement book, but it does allow him to be complicated. He is genuinely, if selfishly, sensitive (the comparison with Ruskin comes into his own mind but is rejected with irritable embarrassment), full of social awkwardness, confused sexual longing, and the melodramatic *Waste Land*ism of his generation: "He thought you make a little circle and yours reflects other circles. Death, death, sackcloth and ashes."[78] What can such a character hope to achieve at a big industrial concern, given new foreign competition, long-standing internal squabbles, and, especially, his father's crushing mixture of neglect and rivalry in his dealings with him? Naturally, he decides to get rid of the old men.

This Oedipal theme is pervasive and is least controlled in scenes concerning Dupret senior. Henry Green scored some crude hits against Vincent Yorke, making his fictional version a capricious tyrant, notoriously mean with money and determined to humiliate his son by allowing him to make changes merely so that he can reverse them, "just to show him."[79] In one of the more reckless touches, Dupret senior falls ill as a result of slipping in dogshit and is subjected to a comic-macabre experiment by Mrs. Dupret, who hires "a well-known courtesan" in an effort to revive him.[80] "Why could not the old man die?" his son wonders frankly and soon has his wish. Elsewhere, however, generational rivalry is used more subtly to link the two worlds of the novel. Halfway through writing it, Henry had told Nevill that "this constant battling with a pattern which is almost geometrical brings me to a finer point . . . than dealing with people."[81] But it is through the people that the patterns are drawn. Dick's contest with his father is echoed in the battle between one of their employees, Gates, and his daughter Lily, which leads to her elopement with Bert Jones. These events are themselves precipitated by the men's new anxieties about forced retirements and reduced working hours—stresses that Dick, in his enthusiasm to take charge, has exacerbated and that lead to a painfully well-depicted atmosphere of conspiracy and mistrust.

None of this is spelled out by Green, who disliked interfering narrators, Greek choruses, and other fictional "know-alls." The writer, he was to say, "has no business with the story he is writing."[82] This self-effacement influenced one of the most often commented-on aspects of the book: its economy with definite articles and other "deictics": *the, this, that.* Apart from echoing the work of C. M. Doughty—who, Green was to write, treated his tales "as a man will granite that he has to fashion"[83]—he wanted to avoid "elegance that is too easy" and was interested in the compactness of Anglo-Saxon poetry and of contemporary Midland speech. The critic Valentine Cunningham has pointed out that there is a revealing contrast between this manner and the style of Lawrence and, later (though he may have been influenced by Green in the 1920s), of Auden, whose excess of demonstratives conveys "an effort to assert authority, knowledge, command of experience."[84]

The distrust conveyed in *Living* of assertiveness of any kind leads to one of its strangest, most moving, and most modern episodes. Lily and Bert are trying to emigrate to Canada via Liverpool, where they hope to get help from Bert's parents. Their journey from Birmingham has been furtive and anxious—comically so: Lily is afraid that attention will be drawn to them by the tulips Bert has given her, so he tries to leave them in the station lavatory, from which "Like old stage joke they were brought to them by lavatory attendant."[85] That night in Liverpool, Lily worries increasingly about having abandoned Mr. Craigan, with whom she and her father lodge. He is one of the factory's old hands, has fallen ill, and is afraid he will be laid off. Bert, meanwhile, is still more anxious about his parents' whereabouts: In his romantic enthusiasm, he hasn't admitted to Lily that he has been out of touch with them for three years and that they may (as it turns out) have moved. This chapter, which brings the end of Lily's and Bert's hopes together, has begun with a Samuel Beckett–like outburst from the storyteller at his inability to help either his characters or his readers:

> What is a town then, how do I know? What did they do? They went by lamps, lamps, lamps, each one with light and dark strung up on it each with streets these were in. Houses made the streets, people made the houses. People lived in them, thousands millions of lives. Each life dully lived and the life next it, pitched

together, walls between built, dully these lives went out onto streets.[86]

Fiction's—and life's—bafflement at how many individuals there are to consider is one of the tragic themes of *Living*. But here the narrative grumbles on with an eccentricity conspicuous even by its own standards: "Procreating was like having a dog, in particular spaniels. Fido who I'm so grateful to."[87] At moments like this, a reader can wonder how much Henry Yorke was in control of Henry Green's writing. There are other puzzles and insecurities—especially, once again, about names: the inclusion, for example, of three characters with overlapping names—Bert Jones, Arthur Jones, and Arthur Bridges—the last of whom, by a still more confusing stroke, is known to his wife as Phil.[88] The narrator rightly worries that we—or he—will not know who some people are, telling us belatedly that "foreman's name was Andrew Philpots" (another echo) and a little farther on, in case we've forgotten, that Andrew "was foreman in iron foundry shop in this factory."[89]

For the reader, there are several possible responses to all this, not mutually inconsistent. The first is quite simply that in the intensity of his responses to individual moments, characters, and situations, Green did sometimes find it difficult to control a whole narrative. He was later to write with awe of Virginia Woolf's "amazing grasp" of construction, "the carrying of the complete projection in the head, a capacity . . . which may only come from long application."[90] And in *Living*, the way that the increasing interest in Lily Gates leads to Dupret's being forgotten by the end does seem unplanned. The second response, Frank Kermode's in *The Genesis of Secrecy*, is that from such difficulties, and the reader's sense of them, flow some of the novels' beauties: "A text with all its wits about it would see and hear and remember too much. . . . There would be no game, only a carnal world and not the blindman's buff of the spirit."[91] The third is that control itself and the difficulty of exerting it, and the question of how far it is anyway desirable, are among the book's preoccupations. Both the narrator's outburst about the intolerable populousness of cities and his apparent confusions over names have direct bearings, after all, on the subject of *Living*: a bewilderingly large urban business and the people who are dependent on that business; how they get their living, how their lives are run, how far they are free to live for themselves; what, if anything, their being alive amounts to. On the first page, Dupret's impressions of the place are overwhelmed (as Lily's of Liverpool will be) by sheer numbers:

> Bridesley, Birmingham.
> Two o'clock. Thousands came back from dinner along streets. . . .
> Thousands came back to factories they worked in from their dinners. . . .
> Hundreds went along road outside, men and girls. Some turned in to Dupret factory.

If Dupret is daunted, the reader can be, too. Whether or not Green knew the book at first hand, it sounds as if he may have been influenced by Friedrich Engels's *The Condition of the Working-Class in England,* with its horrified evocation of an overcrowded urban world: "Hundreds and thousands of men and women drawn from all classes and ranks of society pack the streets. . . . Are they not all human beings with the same innate characteristics and potentialities, all equally interested in the pursuit of happiness? . . . Yet they rush past one another as if they had nothing in common."[92]

In the first twenty-six pages of *Living,* no fewer than twenty-six people have been introduced by name. More come later, among them the foreman, Philpots, whom, as we have seen, the narrative is so concerned not to forget. To himself though, Philpots can be assumed to be memorable enough, and surely it is this that prompts those awkward gestures toward him and the book's avoidance of more conventional introductions. A similar point is made by Lily's question, "We shan't be like the others Bert?"[93] She insists to herself, "I, I am I. I am I," and tries to assert her individuality by her decision to emigrate, which she imagines transfigures her—"every woman she looked at like she was a queen, they her subjects, was an eagle in her eyes."[94] But Dupret, who has just gone past her into the factory, did not notice her, "she was so like the others."[95] It sometimes looks as though there may be a know-it-all behind the narrative, after all: one with an old-fashioned sense of irony.

Anthony Powell wrote later of Green's interest "in the eternal contrast between everyday life's flatness and its intensity,"[96] but they are more interdependent than contradictory. The crowds who so oppress parts of the story also provide some of its consolations: at the football ground, or in the cinema, where "every head . . . tumbled without hats against another."[97] In the same way, the book's many images of escape are tied to its domestic stabilities. Racing pigeons are one example, a trope Green used first in his sketch "Saturday," one of his early attempts to write about Birmingham life.[98] In their inseparable freedom and dependency, the birds are as symbolic of the novel's themes as Chekhov's seagull or Ibsen's wild duck are in their own contexts. Lily watches the pigeons attentively, and when she is abandoned by Bert and goes home to Mr. Craigan, we remember how the moment was anticipated a couple of chapters previously:

> As . . . the housewives on a Sunday will go out, in their aprons, carrying a pigeon and throw this one up and it will climb in spirals up in the air, then, when it has reached a sufficient height it will drop down plumb into the apron she holds out for it, so Miss Gates, in her thoughts . . . was always coming bump back again to Mr. Craigan.[99]

The story's attitude is complex, then, and not least about Lily's return. These Birmingham homes are places where there isn't enough money, men behave tyrannously, women get knocked about; but in them, too, water falling into a basin can become a Matisse vision, and a new baby can explain and justify everything. Some readers are dismayed by the way Lily's stirrings of independence seem to be abandoned in her final lunge at a pram, but what Green was responding to in her was, among other things, her desire for creativity. Children, he argued to a critic of this aspect of the novel, "for that class . . . as of course really for every class, are the only creative thing they can do."[100] *Living* is a book about how people really live: their hopes, but also their compromises and defeats and the way those defeats may not be so bad after all. Green neither romanticizes his proletarian characters nor pretends to hold out radical solutions for them.[101] His narrative asks some fierce questions, but if any of them find an answer it is a resigned "Because, because." The words are those of Mrs. Eames, who lives next door to Craigan and keeps an eye out for him and for Lily. She is talking to her baby, in a wonderfully well-heard episode early in the book, set apart like an island from the no-less-convincing paranoia and betrayals of the factory floor.

> "What will we do with him? Beauty, when you grow to be a man, eh, what will we do with you? . . . sure as anything you'll leave us when you're a man, and who'll we 'ave then, eh cruel? Sons and daughters why do we bring them into the world?" She was laughing. "Because, because" she said laughing and then lay smiling and then yawned.[102]

HAVING FINISHED HIS FIRST DRAFT, HENRY FOR THE first time became doubtful about the book. "I'm violently depressed and have been for the last month or two," he told Anthony Powell in mid-October. "My fucking novel is so absolutely mediocre."[103] It was just as well that he wasn't overconfident about it, because when the manuscript reached Edward Garnett in November, the editor's reaction was mixed:

> Yes, "Living" is very clever. It gains on one, as one reads, & the last third is the best. At first I found the style difficult, & a trifle affected. But one sees afterwards that you wanted to keep the tone & atmosphere free from the middle-class manner of writing! At the same time it is so unusual that the majority of your readers may feel baulked by this manner; & I think you should insert a few descriptive passages, early in the story, so that one may visualize the environment. . . .
>
> You have accomplished a feat in carrying "Living" through; & so far as it goes its admirably true. Only just as there is more in the upper class life than your "interludes" convey so there is more in the working class life than the "conversations" express. But so far as it stretches it's rigorous & exact.
>
> Will you come round some evening for a talk.
>
> *PS* The last third—from the point where the old men are sacked—is damnably good—a fine strong piece of work.[104]

Henry was disappointed that the novel should have seemed "clever." Less reasonably, he was very reluctant to add the kind of descriptive exposition Garnett wanted, which he felt would spoil his symbolic pattern-ing. But the extent of their disagreement over this did not become fully clear until after Christmas.

Meanwhile, Henry avoided the tensions he anticipated at 9 Mans-field Street by planning to spend the holiday with the members of Robert Byron's family, who were in Vienna for a year. When they had left En-gland, he had lamented, "It really is tragic. . . . It is too dreadful to think of. Of course you will never come back. 'The Byrons of Vienna' we shall say with a catch in our voices. 'What do they do there? They live there. They *won't* come back.'"[105] Now, as early as two months before he was due to join them, his letters were already filled with hilarious foreboding and news of mock-elaborate preparations. His grandfather's three fur coats were being taken out of cold storage for him, he claimed, so he would be "quite well off in that respect."[106] He was worried, though, about not speaking German, and about Robert's description of the apartment, which suggested that all the bedrooms opened off one an-other. Perhaps it would be better if he stayed at the Hotel Sacher and simply spent the days and evenings with the Byrons. He looked forward to going to the opera—"I cry & moan . . . dont you, but I enjoy it a good deal"—but was less enthusiastic about plans to go skating.

Although, according to Robert, there was going to be a revolution in Austria, Henry's stay was to be pleasantly peaceful.[107] It was one of the coldest winters of the century, and Henry sat by the stove all day long, chatting happily.[108] The Byrons were all very fond of him, from Robert's mother, Margaret, to his sixteen-year-old sister, Lucy, and in the warmth of the family's admiration Henry relaxed and was amusing. He wrote a whimsical comic sketch for Lucy and a friend to perform, in which a doe and a chicken squabble about the doe's wish to leave Savernake For-est.[109] He had brought the manuscript of *Living* for Mrs. Byron to read—"a great compliment," Robert told her, "as no one else has seen it. . . . I feel rather jealous!!"[110] The following summer, Mrs. Byron wrote to him nostalgically: "My dear Henry, Three *extremely* nice young Ox-ford men came to tea with us yesterday and when they had gone we said what *very* nice men they are, quite charming, *so* pleasant, delightful manners, such typical Englishmen, *so* suitable for the diplomatic service, good figureheads, *so* fluent at German, *so very nice* but oh Lord *so* dull, if only Henry had been here."[111]

He had not entirely forgone the comforts of the Hotel Sacher, spending an evening there with a distant Austrian cousin, Max Thurn, and in general the end of his stay in Birmingham marked the beginning of a glossy, sociable, sophisticated period in his life. He read Henry James, returned to Proust, bought "hundreds of suits" and some Barbizon drawings, and went to see Josephine Baker perform ("extremely beautiful when dancing & quite hideous when still").[112] Despite his continuing argument with Garnett about the early pages of *Living*, he felt confident enough about the book to demand better terms from Dent. He grew ever closer to Dig, telling the rejected Anthony Powell unkindly if somewhat obscurely that both she and Mary seemed "to live by symbols of absolutely hair raising beauty." The immediate future was beginning to look good. "After Christmas," he told Powell buoyantly, "I hope to be in London for ever."[113]

CHAPTER 5

The Bright Young Yorkes

LONDON COULD NOT, OF COURSE, HAVE LIVED UP TO all of his expectations, since they continued to be as divided as his feelings about most things. He was glad to be back in a sophisticated world of parties and jazz, yet on New Year's Day 1929, he wrote Margaret Byron a morning-after account of a visit to a "howling" nightclub full of "old men with red faces & bald heads with their eyes knocking against their spectacles, yelling & shrieking."[1] He enjoyed seeing more of his friends but still ran them down when they were not around. And he both relished and deplored the prosperity of his new surroundings on his daily journey to the office: the mixture of semirural parks and comfortable residential streets, the displays in fashionable shopwindows, the sheer un-Birmingham-like luxury on the eve of depression.

Once again, inconsistency seems to have been a way of leaving himself imaginatively open. He was still working intermittently on "Mood," and although he eventually abandoned it, seen as a prose poem it is complete in its way.[2] Its earlier working title was "Meretricity," a made-up word that suggests electricity as well as meretriciousness—appropriately so, since the story dwells on both the buzz and the deceptiveness of sexual attraction. The main preoccupation is with the psychology of a beautiful, self-absorbed *flâneuse* named Constance, whom we meet in the West End in summer.[3] The narrative, which shows signs of having been influenced by Virginia Woolf's *Mrs. Dalloway*, explores Constance's thoughts as she walks down Oxford Street and the thoughts of an attendant in Hyde Park from whom she rents a deck chair. It involves a kind of voyeurism on the part of narrator and reader: Together, we gaze intently at her and into her at first empty-seeming mind, with all the besottedness of the ticket collector himself, gaping as she rummages in her handbag:

> Standing above her he held the ticket in his fingers and Lord love us he thought if women don't put a lot in there. But he found his eyes followed the line of her left hand which held the bag while she fumbled in it with her right, and if, automatically almost, he kept exclaiming within him at the magnificence of that blue cigarette case and God help us look at that holder, yet the major part of him yearned to an exquisite transparency, like a seashell in the sea, where her thumb branched off from the palm of her hand. Save us, he cried out in his heart, if I couldn't bury my nose in there, such fine hands, never a day's work in their lives and the nails, like a quartz.[4]

This passage comes near the end and forms a climax of sorts to the yearning intrusions that the piece embodies. What precedes it says a lot about Constance, although it might have been thought that there was not much to say. She thinks shallowly about older women, about the south of France, about her childhood in Kent, and as she does so we learn in a short space about her upbringing, which has been not unlike that of Dig and Miss Biddulph. Constance has the gratuitous, unchallengeable beauty of a bird ("She walked exactly like herons fly") or of the tree near her home that "reached out olive-blue branches and poured shade on the ground." The gift is meretricious, or so we are at first led to think, in the sense that it deceives us into supposing that it will be connected with some corresponding moral or intellectual quality. But Constance herself seems to have no such quality. As the narrative opens, she is all selfishness, an overindulged fluctuating mass of mood: This is one of the story's points. Gradually, though, we learn of unexpected depths of feeling, half-concealed hurts that in turn help to explain her moodiness and self-preoccupation. Her great friend Celia has married and, as Constance says to herself in her clichéd, proto–Princess Diana–ish way, "When you have been two you can't be three." So Constance is learning for the first time to be alone. The process of having nobody "so to speak to play with" is itself a route to growing up. She sees it as a source of imaginative strength—even of imaginative necessity, since if a woman's life is "too full," as Constance imagines the married Celia's must be, it leaves too little space for fantasy. In the story's closing words,

> the issue ultimately is with ourselves. As my two eyes are coordinated so let me have myself as my friend, may I have that glory where I draw on no one, lean on nobody. May I learn to be alone.

The plangent note of imaginative independence and lonely individualism is a long way from the vacuity with which Constance's reverie began ("She wondered where that woman bought her sponges. One shouldn't go just anywhere for one's sponge"). And it is not until he has begun to introduce this element that Green brings on the ticket collector, with his own petty preoccupations and resentments. As a result, we take the new character with some seriousness, and the minuscule exchange between him and Constance has an intensity that is startling for the fact that it is felt only partially by either of them, and then in quite different ways. A fiction that seemed far removed from *Living* turns out to have a similar motivating force. People from mutually dependent but, on the surface, utterly divided classes are brought together on the page in a way that makes the reader see each as having equal selfhood.

Meanwhile, Green won his tussle with his publishers over *Living*. Among other things, Edward Garnett had wanted some assistance for readers in keeping all the characters in mind—perhaps a cast list. Green ignored these suggestions and used his holiday in Austria as a delaying tactic.[5] In January 1929, an internal report at Dent complained that Green "has not made the additions . . . that we agreed to" and added that the book's title would be "bad selling" and "must be changed." Despite the author's intransigence, though, and the likelihood that his condensed, elliptical style would "'put off' many readers," the report spoke of the book's "brilliant impressionism" and "astonishing veracity" and concluded that it would be "impossible to pass such a novel over . . . for Mr Green certainly has a future."[6] *Living* was to appear, unaltered, that summer.

Henry's future as a writer now seemed increasingly complicated by his prospects as a businessman. To his family, the latter seemed closely linked to his chances as a husband, with all the steadiness that marriage would, it was hoped, confer on him. Within a few months of Henry's arrival in the London office of Pontifex, Vincent Yorke and John Biddulph were involved in protracted negotiations over a marriage settlement. Henry's net annual salary was £200, but this represented only part of his income. According to the calculations set out between the fathers, he would take a further £500 annually as a share of the firm's profits, plus the proceeds of a trust fund worth at least £600 a year. Dig, meanwhile, would have £300 a year settled on her, which her father offered to increase by £100 if Vincent would match it. These terms brought the young couple's joint prospects to £1,800, and possibly more, since Vincent may have minimized his son's wealth in order to persuade John to improve his offer. Whatever the precise sum, to professional literary people such as Tony Powell and Evelyn Waugh, it seemed a fortune. Powell, recalling the contrast between his position and Henry's, said that "£400 was pretty well-off."[7]

At the time, Henry complained that Vincent was behaving "thoroughly badly & with characteristic dishonesty" and contrasted the mercenary spirit of the negotiations with his own "obsessed & passionate" feelings for Dig.[8] He told Evelyn Waugh, "For the last 10 weeks I've been reminded every day how the Russians in their writings understated all the fantastic scenes of private life."[9] Even allowing for his usual exaggeration, it is clear that he was under some strain. "I'm in a very weak state of health & nerves," he confided lugubriously to Robert Byron. "I've even taken to crying every now & again." The settlement was concluded in April 1929,[10] to the undisguised relief of Henry's parents (Maud told Maurice Bowra, "I wouldn't have minded almost anyone, except of course a Roman Catholic"),[11] and Henry found himself swept into respectability. Robert Byron described a dinner party at which he was amazed to find his friend with his "hair brushed and accepting invitations to all kinds of dances!!"[12] The usually unkempt Henry complained a good deal about having to look tidy and be polite to all the family, especially all his aunts. He had never dreamed, he told Ottoline Morrell, that being engaged was so exhausting: "Buying a top hat is absolutely hellish."[13]

He revenged himself for some of the strain by giving a newspaper interview. Hitherto, the fact that the novelist Henry Green had anything to do with the Yorkes, let alone the Wyndhams, had not been widely known. Of itself, the revelation was hardly startling, but his parents detested publicity of any sort. They had managed to keep Gerald's affair out of the papers, only to see Henry, in all his naïve garrulity, blazoned across the *Star*.[14] The piece was headed AUTHOR'S WORK AS FACTORY HAND, but it was the subheadings that grated most: "Lord Leconfield's Nephew Finds 'Local Colour'"; "Bored with Oxford"; "Pals Among the Men"; "Woman Who Pitied Him." The last phrase introduced a jaunty anecdote about his excursion into poverty. "I used to be covered in dirt," Henry was reported to have said, "and my overalls were torn and burnt with acids. . . . Once, while shopping in a small street in Birmingham . . . I heard the woman behind the counter say 'I'll bet he is a public school boy. I wonder what has brought him to this.'" He confided that he had kept his overalls. "I have them at home now as a souvenir, and hope one day to be able to go back to the factory."

Adding to the general embarrassment, Henry was described "sitting in his comfortable study in an old-world house off one of London's quiet squares," where he chattered on complacently about his father's firm. "I was treated exactly like the other employees. At first I was paid £1 a week, and at the end of three years I rose to 30 s[hillings]. . . . And the men, I loved them. They are fine fellows, generous, open-hearted, and splendid pals. . . . Of course, they knew who I was, but that made no difference." He added helpfully, "My father and mother have a country house not far from Birmingham."

Henry took a good deal of adolescently subversive pleasure in his parents' reaction. "That interview you saw I gave in the paper has been the cause of endless trouble," he told Evelyn Waugh. "My family rave with fury about it, even when they go to the lavatory I can hear the moans escaping from their mouths over it, between the stertorous breathing & volleys of farts. They produced an ultra snobbish line about it & gave themselves away a good deal."[15] But as usual his rebelliousness was mingled with more caution than he liked to admit. His and Dig's wedding was held at Saint Margaret's, Westminster. Though the late July day was blazingly hot, he not only wore his top hat but carried a rolled umbrella.

Apart from Gerald's presence (as Henry's best man), the arrangements could not have been more conventional. Dig wore a cream tulle dress embroidered with diamanté and carried a vast bouquet dominated by blue delphiniums.[16] The whole family turned out: Leconfields, Maxses, Wyndhams, the countess of Hardwicke, Lady Olein Quinn, and many others, as well as friends such as Robert Byron, John Sutro, and Nancy Mitford and her future brother-in-law Esmond Romilly. The reception was held at the Biddulphs' London house at 36 Lowndes Square, Knightsbridge. Retainers from the Biddulph and Yorke estates were entertained in a separate room.

The couple took a boat train to Var, near Saint Tropez. Dig was exhausted, but once she had rested they were "frightfully well & happy & quite unequal to writing letters."[17] In honor of their surroundings, Henry dared to buy a red shirt,[18] and one evening Dig persuaded him to dance, having chosen "a very obscure café in the village for the event." She reported in a letter to her "darling cousin Maud" (Henry's mother) that although Henry danced well, he complained that it made him giddy and refused do it at the hotel.[19] The honeymooners fantasized about their fellow guests, went for aimless walks along the coast, admired the landscape, deplored the number of sketchers, and bathed twice a day on a quiet beach.[20]

IN SEPTEMBER THE COUPLE WAS BACK IN LONDON and living on the north side of Hyde Park, staying briefly in Gloucester Square before they settled in a solid Regency house on the adjoining Radnor Place, where they began to try to learn about domesticity. Despite Henry's fascination with servants, he and Dig were bad at employing them. Within weeks, the cook gave notice. Two days later, Dig had to have her tonsils out, so Henry was left to interview candidates for the cook's job, all of whom he suspected of being either drunkards or thieves.[21] Once Dig was better and the servant problem had been temporarily solved, the Yorkes' date books filled up again. Ever since their engagement, they had been seen everywhere, from a public dinner at which Henry, in his new managerial role, was implausibly joined as a speaker by the minister of health and the general manager of the Metropolitan Railway, to an 1860s party given by the Bryan Guinnesses, at which Dig appeared as a ballerina, she-Evelyn Waugh as a little boy in trousers, rolling a hoop, and Nancy Mitford as her ancestress Lady Georgiana Mitford. Tom Mitford came in drag.[22] Henry's apparel is not recorded. But whatever they were wearing, Henry and Dig were easy on the eye and amusing to be with, and as time went by they were taken up by some glamorous new friends, among them the Ruthven twins— upper-class girls who had become music-hall stars—and the Aga Khan's son Aly and his mistress, Peggy Harmsworth. In January 1930, Evelyn Waugh gave a dinner at Boulestin's to celebrate the publication of *Vile Bodies*.[23] Harold Acton, Nancy Mitford, and Rebecca West were among the guests, along with the couple whom Waugh, parodying the society columnists, now called "the bright young Yorkes" or alternatively, "Mr H. Yorke the lavatory king and his pretty wife."[24]

While Henry's job was much mocked, it added to the aura of originality that surrounded him. Anthony Powell remembers, perhaps a shade enviously, that everyone went around saying "Henry is a sort of Goethe, you know—writes novels and is frightfully good at business."[25] ("The artist as businessman" was to be the subject of a sardonic comment by one of the characters in *A Dance to the Music of Time*: "I never pay my insurance policy . . . without envisaging the documents going through the hands of Aubrey Beardsley and Kafka, before being laid on the desk of Wallace Stevens."[26]) Despite popular rumor among Henry's friends—based on the all-too-widespread evidence of Pontifex "No Sound" Syphon Cisterns and Pontifex-Emmanuel toilet bowls—lavatories were not, in fact, the main line of the firm, which they nicknamed Pontifex Maximus. The plumbing side was run by Vincent Yorke's younger brother, Ralph, as a separate business named Shanks. Pontifex's chief product was a high-pressure filling machine for beer bottling, which enabled Gerald to joke that the company catered to people's needs at both ends. In the 1930s, most big towns had their own small brewery, and most small breweries bought their filling machines and other equipment from Pontifex. Vincent still kept tight control of the business. Henry now often accompanied him on his regular trips to Birmingham and was also expected to keep him closely informed of developments when Vincent's other business concerns took him abroad.[27] The deals involved were often large. In May 1930, for example, Henry wrote to Vin-

think of anyone who managed to be "so egotistical, yet so nice" as she was.[27] He remembered her brother with less affection, describing him as a bully, "incapable of forming relationships"—except with literature, which Spender acknowledged John Lehmann loved and promoted zealously. John had been a younger contemporary of Henry at Eton, where he coedited *College Days,* and he had become a major literary entrepreneur.[28] As a poet, he had found his first publishers and, simultaneously, his first employers in Virginia and Leonard Woolf at the Hogarth Press, had spent much of the 1930s in Vienna, where he became an impresario of the European literary left, and in 1936 began the magazine *New Writing.* Henry Green was not among the journal's first contributors, but W. H. Auden and Christopher Isherwood were, and they told John Lehmann how much they admired Green's work.[29] It was Rosamond, though, together with Goronwy Rees, who persuaded Henry to offer *Party Going* to Hogarth after Dent had turned it down. When the Woolfs hesitated over it, John suggested sending the manuscript to Christopher Isherwood for comment. Isherwood's enthusiasm won the day.[30] Green's arrival on the Hogarth Press list seemed to Lehmann to represent "a new phase" in the firm's development.[31] Given the long gestation of *Party Going,* he could scarcely have anticipated how productive this phase was going to be for its author.

THE NOVEL WAS CRITICALLY WELL RECEIVED. HENRY was as glum about good reviews as about bad ones, commenting to John Lehmann that it was odd that they "never sell books" and warning him that neither of his previous novels had done well commercially.[32] Still, *Party Going* sold respectably for the time—1,285 copies in the first twelve months—and made a small profit for the publishers.[33] Once again, Green's friends had done their best for him. Auden and Isherwood gave *Party Going* a jointly written prepublication puff in *Vogue,*[34] and the novelist and critic David Garnett, son of Henry's first editor, described it very quotably in the *New Statesman* as "screamingly funny," "the perfectly inappropriate book for the times," one that might have been written by Groucho Marx if he had fallen under the spell of Virginia Woolf and sat down to write a novel about the rich.[35] Green "knows altogether too much about young women," Garnett wrote, while finding that elements in the book were almost surgically shrewd and detached, a quality that was to be still more evident in Green's memoir, *Pack My Bag,* a draft of which he put into Rosamond's hands almost as soon as *Party Going* appeared.

Few autobiographers (though Cyril Connolly ran close) have been so unsparing of themselves, so free from self-aggrandizement. The author's snobbery, opportunism, self-doubt, even cowardice are laid bare with a kind of naïve embarrassment. The mood, in his own words, is "shame remembered"—which would have made a good title, though Henry was as uncertain about what to call it as he had been earlier about what to call himself. He suggested "Self-Portrait," "Henry Green by Henry Green," and "Before a War" but was finally persuaded to use the dying words of the philosopher F. H. Bradley, which in their new context hinted at wartime exigencies as well as picking up a morbid strain that runs through the book.[36] Lehmann—perhaps influenced by the success of what had been mistaken for escapism in *Party Going*—thought the doom-laden aspect of the manuscript "a bit silly."[37] The first paragraph refers to the need to record "before one is killed," and this note is re-echoed often and with increasing extravagance as the book nears its end. Green is writing, he repeats, "to wake what is left of things remembered into things to die with." "We who must die soon," he says, "should chase our memories back"; "death in my case I am afraid will come too soon"; "interest in what goes on about us has been sharpened by the fear of death"—an eventuality likely to result from "fighting for something which, as I am now, for the life of me I cannot understand."[38] All this is in counterpoint to the clear-eyed and often comic memories that the book relates, though even here everything looks ahead to present circumstances. In a description of fox hunting, the huntsman's horn is linked, as in a movie sound track, to air-raid sirens being tried out in London. In another passage, novelist and managing director merge when the author describes prewar Britain as a business in the receiver's hands, its people taking a last look at the forfeited goods.

Green was preoccupied by the unreliability of such stocktaking, by the fictional character of all self-description. Some of the book's frankness is attributable to this. "What a merciless eye he has for human behaviour!" John Lehmann wrote to Rosamond, "and how unexpected and fascinating his metaphors nearly always are!" She relayed the words to Henry but without the "nearly," which was in fact very much to the point.[39] Green's determination to be guileless, combined with the speed with which he wrote the book, produces some odd effects. There are failures of tone and argument that the Lehmanns could easily have edited out—especially the book's vacillations between class guilt and flagrant snobbery.[40] But Henry had convinced everyone that it was important to capitalize on the success of *Party Going* and, spurred by a penalty clause in his contract which required an additional payment of fifty pounds if the book had not appeared by Christmas 1940 and a further fifty if it was delayed beyond the following May, Hogarth pushed it through by the earlier date.[41] However unsatisfactory the unevenness of *Pack My Bag* can sometimes seem, ambivalence is part of its essence—so much so that when the poet and novelist Richard Church reviewed it, he did so twice, giving opposite verdicts, first in *John O'London's Weekly,* where he praised both Green's earlier books and the autobiography ("I strongly recommend it") for their courage, originality, and honesty; then, two weeks later, railing in the *Spectator* that "both in this book and in his earlier attempts at the art of the novel, I can see no excuse for this infantilism. . . . Perhaps he is aping that school of painters which is already outmoded, who drew profile portraits with two eyes."[42] (When Lehmann remonstrated with him for what must rank among the quickest volte-faces in the history of literary criticism, Church said blithely that he was writing for two different kinds of reader "and thus gave bent [*sic*] to both sides of my own reaction to the book. I liked it and I didn't like it, and I had to say so.")[43]

In truth, it is not always easy to see where Green's bold expressions of dividedness are not simply sheer confusion. As Church noted, the mixture is most evident at a stylistic level, in the wider than usual gap between the uncalculated-seeming talking voice ("everything must go down that one can remember, all one's tool box, one's packet of Wrigley's") and sudden, beautiful gusts of lyricism, as in the passages about fishing or about Gerald.[44] But there is a deeper, less obtrusive ambiguity in the final, memorably tender passage about Henry and Dig's epistolary courtship and the fact that "for the ten years now we have not had to write because we are man and wife, there was love."[45]

Perhaps not too much should be made of that slide of tense from *are* to *was*. Green was uninterested in—indeed, consciously against—grammatical correctness for its own sake.[46] But there's a related, Beckettian uncertainty in the words that come immediately before, describing the escape out of childhood into "life itself at last in loneliness certainly at first." One way of reading this is to interpret "loneliness . . . at first" as having been cured by Dig. But "at last in loneliness" carries a hint of finality, even of vindication, which picks up several earlier hints in the book—most obviously in his descriptions of his solitude at Forthampton when his brothers had gone away to school and at Eton when Gerald had left for Cambridge.[47] Nowhere is this sense of isolation sharper than in a reference to his brother Philip's funeral, where Green talks of how the church is involved "in all those few moments when we stand alone, at birth, in marriage, and at death."[48] If marriage had come to seem a form of solitude to Henry, war promised the opposite. It was an event that brings "strangers to conversation with each other"[49]—strangers who, in Henry's case, included men in the Fire Service and several young women, some of whom were engaged on war work. One of the latter became a spy. Another has remained a mystery.

The mobilization of hundreds of thousands of men in their late teens and early twenties gave those of Henry's generation a sense of aging that was all the more acute for being premature. Evelyn Waugh's fictional alter ego, Guy Crouchback, is nicknamed "Uncle" by the young officers in his regiment, and the thirty-five-year-old author of *Pack My Bag* is similarly conscious that youth has suddenly passed: "a change of wind and the boat is blown in, there is nothing to do but tie up and call it a day."[50] One consequence of such reflections was the widespread impulse to write memoirs: John Lehmann's magazine *New Writing* became dominated by autobiographical pieces.[51] Another, for which there was plenty of opportunity in the inaction of the "Phoney" or "Bore" War, in 1939–early 1940, was falling in love with much younger women.

One of these in Henry's case was Ann Glass, a teenage debutante at the beginning of the war, precocious, clever, beautiful, and funny.[52] She had already been to finishing schools in Italy and Germany and to the Webber Douglas drama school when Henry Yorke met her at Peggy Harmsworth's house. A year later, he bumped into her on Bond Street and told her, "You are now old enough for me to ask you out." She was old enough, too, to have been recruited by MI5, while still easily young enough to combine this day job with a full-time nocturnal social life. Her parents had taken a room for her in the Dorchester Hotel, which had exceptionally deep air-raid shelters and was convenient to Whitehall.[53] She was rarely there. Henry was one of many admirers—they were to include the war correspondent Charles Collingwood and the American diplomat Dorsey Fisher—but for a year from November 1940, at the height of the Blitz, they saw a great deal of each other. When Henry had time off after a night shift, he and Ann often spent all day together before going to the Ritz Bar for drinks, to Belle Meunière for dinner, and on to a nightclub.[54] For part of that winter, Ann was on an assignment at Blenheim Palace, and she and Henry became familiar with the timetable of the early-morning milk trains between Paddington and Oxford.[55] Her letters from Woodstock are full of nostalgia for times they spent together at clubs in the West End: "Oh, if only we were back in the Lansdowne or the Conga or a sort of heavenly mixture of both, suspended above time in a golden dream of swing and brandy and enchanted conversation."[56] Henry gave his own version of their idyll in a story that George Orwell admired, "The Lull," which contains a flashback in which "a fireman in mufti and a young girl" spend a summer afternoon by the Serpentine, where she recites French love poetry to him and reproaches him for being "the worst-read man I've ever met."[57]

Often, the boundary wars found in most romances broke out. He took fright when she telephoned him at home on the night of a particularly heavy raid on London;[58] she reproved him for going too far in a movie theater.[59] There were outbreaks of jealousy about other women, especially a Rosemary Clifford, who evidently reciprocated this feeling.[60] Next to nothing is known about Clifford, and it is hard to reconstruct her relationship with Henry, though it seems a fair guess that she lies behind the Rose who is an object of obsession in his 1945 novel, *Back,* and she may also have been the model for Hilly in *Caught,* a Women's Auxiliary Fire Service (WAFS) girl with whom the central character has an affair. For a while, Clifford either worked at or had access to the Davies Street fire station.[61] Later, she moved, possibly to Whitehall, where, it seems, she missed their previous reckless intimacy—"it's like swimming in a stagnant pond when you've been used to the sea."[62] Rosemary feared Ann's hold over Henry and was determined to assert her own claims. In November 1940, for example, she wrote to thank him for *Pack My Bag:* "Darling, This is very tiresome having to write because I can't put it beautifully like Miss Glass, but you know if I tried to tell you I should have to put my head in a pillow & become embarrassed."[63] Not too embarrassed, though, to ask, "Would you like to know how you look when you're asleep? Your face loses all its creases & becomes very serene." Another tender note establishes a similar intimacy under the guise of an apology for the fact that she has lost Henry's suspenders.[64] He has telephoned her but missed her, so she has tried to imagine him by climbing onto her roof on Park Street, behind Park Lane, where "I think I smelt your hair" on the east wind. The suspenders, she guesses, are in her cupboard "with innumerable tins of prawns we keep for emergency, or else in the box with my bathing suit—I've looked in all likely places." But she still has his Bovril and his space heater. She ends with whimsical fondness, "Have I told you I miss you? because I do—which is a nuisance. If we should meet again—I'm dark & rather grubby —X Rosemary."

Gradually, she came to expect more of him. The letters that Henry kept include one that was typed in a simple code.[65] Though bundled together with those from Ann Glass, it is signed with an initial *R* in a hand that seems to be Clifford's. The author talks about the efforts she has made "tobe ready proyou superweekend," despite her job and also the domestic subterfuges involved. She continues sadly:

> your advise [*sic*] was badly needed para meant to write before but its been desperate time dash kind friendly word exyou would have been great moral support stop para nonangry though sad you make uneffort stop have invested so much youwise that though dont really expect dividends eye cannot let capitol [*sic*] investment disappear altogether stop para make unsuggestions incase you prefer this way nonseeing me dash but pleased see hear if you wish stop love R.

It is not known what happened to Clifford, except that she continued to live in Bayswater at 48 Burnham Court, Moscow Road, and that she was on the list of those to whom Henry asked his publishers to send copies of *Back* in 1946, but by the time of his next publication, in 1950, she was not. Glass, on the other hand, became a good friend—a process in which friendship with Dig, too, was again an outcome. When she married and had a son, Henry was one of his godfathers.

There were many other women friends. Henry had grown ever closer to Mary Strickland after the death of her husband, Tom, in 1938 and Tom's sister's suicide.[66] It is clear from his letters that as the war developed, and with it new relationships, he felt guilty about not giving her as much support as she wanted—and perhaps had grown used to—from him.[67] He lamented—possibly with Dig in mind as much as Mary herself—that it was hard to keep feelings alive at a time of separation, "romantically idiotically trying to keep in touch with what used to be and is still but, don't you agree, is so madly remote under the threat of death & certainly under the forced divorce we live through by reason of our interrupted lives. . . . So you see or don't you?"[68] Whatever Mary saw, Henry's interrupted life did not prevent him from arranging a ride on a fire engine for Pauline Gates, wife of his brilliant friend and business rival Sylvester Gates, or from going to nightclubs *à deux* with her or other women—telling any husbands, "I'm taking your wife to a nightclub and I'll bring her back probably in tatters in the morning."[69] They all assumed that they might at any time be killed by a bomb and would ask each other, "Who are you going out with tonight, darling? Is it someone you want to die with?"[70] No one minded the thought of dying with Henry, who seems to have encouraged the idea. Certainly, his writing was stimulated not only by the thought that it might be the last work he would do but also by the enthusiasm of his nubile new readers. He boasted to John Lehmann about a lipstick mark on the typescript of one story, "Mr Jonas."[71] (It is still there.)

In time, he began to worry about the effects of his social life: "Dropped writing for a bit," he wrote Lehmann in a postscript to a letter dated July 1941. "Seeing too many people."[72] This was about a month after Germany's invasion of the Soviet Union had brought an end to ten months of bombing raids on London and other British cities. The catalog of those desperate nights sits strangely with the story of Henry's private life, so far as it can be pieced together. One of Ann Glass's complaints about his attentions to Rosemary Clifford, for example, is dated

14 November 1940. That night, the Luftwaffe was to destroy Coventry. Three days earlier, twenty-five people had been killed in a printing works on Great Peter Street, Westminster, close to the Houses of Parliament.[73] Nancy Mitford was in London then, living at her parents' house on the some road as Henry, and wrote dryly to a friend:

> Do you want to hear of a few more ruins? Well that pretty Naval & Military [Club] in Piccadilly, also the little church (St James's) there. About 6 new ones in the Row [Rotten Row] which bounced us rather & 2 in Prince's Gate. One very near the Oratory in the B[rompton] road. Dolphin Square (several). All these in the last week except the church. Green St is a fearful mess, Gt Cumberland Place utterly wiped out also those houses, Connaught Place I think it was called facing the Park, very pretty. . . . I *should* enjoy showing you the sights so do come soon.[74]

The Luftwaffe's bombs rained down elsewhere, too—on Birmingham, Southampton, Bristol, Liverpool, Sheffield, Swansea, Portsmouth. But London was always a main target. After seeing Ann onto the milk train back to Oxford on 20 December 1940, Henry was caught up in the chaos made by a single vast explosion that caused structural damage over a half-mile radius in Chelsea: One warden reported that it sounded "as though they had dropped a *train*."[75] On 10 January, Henry and Ann had dinner in London ("Heaven to see you, and heaven to go out together again," Ann wrote afterward). She got back to Oxford at 8:30 in the morning. That night, a big, perhaps armor-piercing bomb penetrated five stories of a warehouse in Covent Garden, eventually exploding beneath its air-raid shelter, onto which the entire building collapsed inward, fracturing a gas main. Incendiary bombs followed. Twenty people died inside while the various would-be helpers—firemen, ambulance drivers, the Heavy Rescue Service, the Women's Voluntary Services, the Incident Inquiry Point—stood by helplessly. "That was a powerless night for those standing, trying, failing," Henry's friend William Sansom recorded.[76] No emotional incandescence could have matched such surroundings. Houses left empty by their owners suddenly erupted into flames as long-smoldering incendiaries took hold; mountains of shattered glass turned roads and pavements into Arctic seascapes; at night, pinpricks of light wavered as people groped through the blackout.[77]

Henry's feelings for Dig remained untouched through all this, and he continued his affectionate reports to friends of what he described as "her own special superb remarks"—for example, when someone told her that antiaircraft gunners seemed unable to hit their targets, she replied, "It seems so *gauche.*"[78] But he kept her at what was in more than one sense a safe distance, sending her letters that implored "DON'T COME UP TO LONDON" and indulging in the heartless practical joke of telephoning her to say he was in a burning building and unlikely to emerge alive.[79]

The dangers were real enough, of course, as well as the mere discomforts. Firemen "got wetter than they had ever thought a man could be," William Sansom wrote.[80] Fighting any fire

> soaks the fireman to the skin in the first five minutes. Often then, in the cold of that winter, he was called upon to fight, wet and frozen, for a stretch of some fifteen hours without respite. Throughout this time he was the special target of the high explosives that were sent down to stir up the fire; he could not think of cover; the nature of the job kept him out in the open or up against the fire. It is, too, a particular tradition with London's firemen that they should attack the fire first from *within* the building. . . . Thus, many of the hours of bombardment were spent enclosed with the dark smoke and the fire between walls dangerously unstable, vulnerable both to the heat of the fire and the shaking up of a nearby bomb.

Westminster presented particular hazards and challenges: buildings that were highly flammable, such as the Palmolive works, and ones that were exceptionally tall or of national importance. There was the behavior of different materials under heat: steel girders that expanded, buckled, and split their surrounding concrete; the peculiarities of various kinds of brick; the propensity of large pieces of ancient stone masonry to crash down from above; live electric cables; exploding bottles; the clouds of hot steam sent back from the fireman's own hose; the sudden loss of the

water supply itself when a bomb cracked a main pipe. And the sheer at-
trition of carrying around hard, densely woven canvas hoses attached to
fittings made of solid brass. Henry was in the thick of all this—not least
in a dangerous rescue that he carried out with another fireman, an ex-
butler named Charlie Vincent, outside John Lewis's in Oxford Street, for
which he felt they should have been decorated but that in the event
earned them a reprimand for not wearing the approved breathing apparatus.[81]

It is not surprising, then, that the Blitz stories that Henry began to
contribute to John Lehmann's magazine *Penguin New Writing* func-
tioned "at full tilt," as John Updike was to write, "bringing to the in-
ferno of blitzed London a descriptive power of almost lurid virtuosity."[82]
This does justice to one aspect—the aspect most like Updike's own style.
Green brilliantly rendered the audiovisual extravagance of the Blitz: the
sky like "one vast corridor down which, with the speed of light, blue
double wooden doors as vast were being slammed in turn"; a high building's top floors, which "with abandon, in recklessness, with fierce ac-
ceptance had exchanged their rectangles for tiger-striped hoops, great
wind-blown orange pennants, huge yellow cobra tongues of flame."[83]
But experiences like this were, as the work of painters such as Leonard
Rosoman shows, the *objets trouvés* of a situation in which incendiary
bombs, high explosives, flares, and moving searchlights were all the illu-
mination of an otherwise blacked-out city. More uncommon is Green's
attention to the prosaic details of the job and its lesser motivations: the
mechanics of ladders, ropes, and water pressures; the proto-absurdist
rhythms of people's gossip as they hang around waiting for something to
happen;[84] their fearful pleasure in safe tasks such as pumping out flood-
water from a deep basement shelter.[85] These flatnesses, the expression of
the idea that bathos is much truer to life than pathos, are what Green
was aiming for. Around this time he wrote an essay on C. M. Doughty
for *Folios of New Writing* in which he implicitly compared Doughty's
Arabian travels with the first wartime experience of writers of Green's
own generation. Doughty is praised for his resistance to predictable effects, to "elegance that is too easy." "There are no petty discoveries in his
travels," only a determination to use "words that exactly describe." Current circumstances might similarly be turned to the advantage of writers,

Green suggested, in forcing them "to go out into new territories, it may well be at home, which they would never otherwise have visited" and thence "towards a style which, by the impact of a life strange to them" would somehow make their work more distinctive and durable. If this happened, it would not be because of novelty in itself, but because new experience made old habits of style impossible and reminded writers of their primary obligation, which Green summarized by quoting Henry James's famous words about "the effort really to see and really to represent." One of the outcomes in Doughty's case, he argued, is that he does not turn people into heroes.[86]

Green's work can sometimes seem inconsistent with this manifesto. In "The Old Lady," a roughly contemporaneous story that John Lehmann rejected, Henry used the romantic exoticism of the *Arabian Nights* as a frame for the Blitz. The narrator has been reading the book in French at his fire station, and it is through it that he sees the ensuing air raid:

> All of a sudden there was a tremendous burst of fire . . . and I looked up and saw three jewels that swayed down, white diamonds that barely dropped, offerings brilliant but aloof . . . three more than gems the ifrit in a roll of drums was letting a breeze carry us . . . three stars the djinn had plucked down from heaven, three flares.[87]

But all this is at odds with the story's center: a casual sexual encounter in an air-raid shelter, witnessed by the narrator while an old man dies outside and an old woman passes by, "never looking up." The episode reappears in Green's next novel, *Caught,* but with its exotic, fantastic ornamentation removed.[88] Green was later to say that one of the major influences on his work had been Céline, who had written in *Journey to the End of the Night* that recording the worst one has seen "without changing one word" is "work enough for a lifetime."[89] Green's bleak account of Second World War London has something in common with Céline's of Paris in 1914–1918, with its focus on cowardice, looting, and sexual license. In *Caught,* he came closer than any other English writer of the time to the shocked verisimilitude of poets of the First World War.

THROUGHOUT *CAUGHT*, THE STORY VEERS BETWEEN the hallucinatory and the humdrum. One of its germs was a disciplinary case in which Henry Yorke served as a witness. A fireman was alleged to have behaved improperly by trying to secure a new job for someone in the service with whom he was having an affair. Legally speaking, his offense was that he had misused stationery belonging to the London County Council—notepaper headed with the address of the Central Fire Station at Isleworth, in Middlesex, on which, in November 1941, he had written the incriminating words "Now Darling how are you. You really are just the Person required. But transfers are rather difficult; but who knows."

It was a relatively quiet period. In June 1941, Germany had turned its main aggression against its ally, Russia. The London Blitz was over for now, and Fire Service officials had more time to give to minor disciplinary matters. With its confusion of romantic values and official ones ("just the Person required"), the situation had an imaginative resonance particularly audible to Henry Yorke, and it augmented the more directly autobiographical material that he brought to the novel. The main character, Richard Roe, comes from a big country house where his young son is spending the war. The novel is dedicated to Sebastian Yorke, who was seven in 1941, and some of the subtlest episodes concern the relations between father and son, which on the father's side have been made more tender by the war. The poignant early pages show them together in the garden of the house in which Richard grew up, Christopher taking his father's hand, then running ahead, Richard slightly isolated by deafness and regretting that in the reserved English way of the time he has "made a point of not kissing" his son.[90] Death is ordinarily omnipresent in these rural surroundings: They find a dead mouse, a trap for rooks, a sick deer. But there are new elements. As Christopher wonders whether the deer will die, a warplane passes overhead. In the background, complexly interwoven in the book's fluid time scheme, there are losses. One comes in a strange episode in which, shortly before the war, Christopher was abducted from a department store by a madwoman. Another is the recent death of his mother.

From this preliminary setting, the narrative moves with Richard back into his fire station: a place of petty resentments, rivalry, and mistrust, especially between the regular firemen and the newcomers; a place, too, of jokes and unexpected loyalties; and a place of claustrophobic low-grade intensity in which other lives are revealed. The cook has a daughter whose husband neglects her and who is suffering from a post-partum depression that leads her to hoard useless things. This links her to Christopher, with his cupidity in the toy shop—"the world his need had made"—and also to the now institutionalized woman who abducted him and who, it transpires, is the sister of the fire-station chief, Pye.

Pye's strange, forced proximity to Roe is emphasized by the fact that their names are adjacent letters in the Greek alphabet—and together, of course, they mean *fire*.[91] Here, as in other ways, Green's unenchanted yet affectionate social realism is screwed up into something more artificial and also harsher. *Caught* is an uncomfortable book, not least in its exploration of the difficulties of conveying or just grasping the truth and people's many reasons, conscious or not, for failing to do so. In the obsessive gossip of the fire station during the months leading up to war and of the phony war itself, most of the characters either misinterpret or deliberately falsify both others and themselves. Pye tries to conceal the existence of his sister and pretends to himself that she isn't crazy at all. (A possibility that he himself may be to blame for her condition is even more deeply buried throughout much of the novel.) The cook deceives herself and others about her attempted confrontation with her daughter's runaway husband. And although, in circumstances like those of the real-life case in which Henry Yorke was involved, the cook got her job at the suggestion of a fireman who is a personal friend, Roe seems to have no evidence for his suggestion that they are having an affair.

Among exaggerations, inventions, and cover-ups, the narrative wanders in a fatalistically corrective mood: "She was, of course, hopelessly wrong in this"; "But he was wrong"; "In this the men were wrong." Green claimed to dislike too-knowing storytellers, but what he really distrusted was omnipotence, not omniscience. He knows what his people are doing but knows, too, that in an imaginatively truthful story, they can't be saved from it. If few works of fiction have been quicker than *Caught* to point out their own ironies, few, either, have allowed sympathetic characters to be simultaneously so craven: It is one of the ways in which it develops the insights of *Pack My Bag.* Richard Roe buys favor with his fellow firemen. He pimps for them. He spreads gossip. He looks for his own immediate professional advantage even in his relationship with the WAFS girl, Hilly. Graham Greene did not admit so unheroic a hero into *Ministry of Fear,* his novel set in the Blitz and published at the same time as *Caught,* in June 1943;[92] though Maurice Bendrix, in *The End of the Affair,* runs close. Both Greene and Elizabeth Bowen, in *The Heat of the Day* (written largely during the war, though not published until 1949), use wartime London as a background for psychopolitical melodrama, for treason and high speeches. When their central characters behave badly, it is on a grand scale. No such protection is afforded to Richard Roe. Even his courage is motivated by fear of being thought incompetent, and what seems to stir him most is the opportunity for voyeurism when he finds the rapt couple in the air-raid shelter.

Artistic honesty of this sort does not come without a struggle—one that Henry Green did not always win. Some of the jokes go on too long. The more melodramatic aspects of the book are unconvincing, especially Pye's encounter with a psychologist and his fear that as a young man he may have had sex with his sister without realizing who she was. There is Green's usual slapdashness about detail (is Ilse Norwegian or Swedish? He suggests both).[93] But in the process of reading, these inchoate elements come to seem a part of the confusion of war itself. Unlike Bowen with her deft but traditional narrative fluency, or Greene with his sensational sideshows, Henry Green refuses to let himself fall back on "artistry" or "effects." In this, the writer closest to him was his protégé James Hanley, whose *No Directions* was published that year as well. Hanley's book has been well described by Robert Hewison: "The physical effects of the Blitz are filtered through the emotional states of the characters, drunk, frightened, ill, old, who only comprehend part of what is going on. But the result is a convincing picture of . . . surreal horror and muddle."[94] *Caught,* though, is far the more complex book. It is also much more readable than it can sound, and often very funny—the firemen's cockroach race, the man with the catchphrase from *King Kong,* the Keystone Kops–ish absurdity of Richard's first fire, when the two regular firemen charge up the stairs of the wrong house and the auxiliaries drive back without them.[95] And these echoes of particular films are matched by a calculatedly cinematic vividness in the narrative cutting, especially in the central section with its interlaced duets—Roe and Hilly; Pye and Prudence; Piper (another fireman) and Mary Howells, the cook; Mary's daughter Brid and her lost husband. Above all, though, the novel makes the reader both curious about and fond of its erratic main character, through whom the tragic futility of war is revealed in the stupendous last section.

Roe is sent home, shocked by blast and exhausted by nine continuous weeks of fire fighting. Wandering up and down the garden with his sister-in-law, Dy, while Christopher runs around playing, Roe gives a halting, obsessive account of the first big raid he faced, in which, it turns out, two of the firemen we have come to know were killed. His story—the only part of the book that describes military action—is intercut with a more full-blown third-person narrative descant, or Greek chorus, in which the spectacular, less prosaic aspects are filled out. In this way, Roe's frustrated, dejected memories of general chaos and panic are qualified by another view, in which people—including, despite his self-castigation, Roe himself—are seen to have acted bravely in an uncontrollable situation: a massive dockland lumberyard on fire, the flames spreading to ships moored in the river, scores of separate fire-fighting units racing around with no intercommunications and no effective overall command, enemy bombers still arriving in waves, water supplies cut off, hoses shredded, pigeons catching fire in the air. This agonizing double narrative—"simply repeatedly plain, the truth, over and over again," as the book earlier described the song of a nightclub musician heard by Roe and Hilly[96]—has to contend with Dy's mixed reactions: boredom, distraction, and, despite her attempts at sympathy, her instinctive resistance to any show of feeling. At one point, she gives Roe a pat, but when tears fill his eyes she briskly withdraws. Alongside them, Christopher carries on his separate but not unrelated imaginative life of violent military fantasies, ironically dreaming himself as what his father has been defending him from.

These final twenty-five pages, with their symphonic emotional and thematic range, are impossible to do justice to in selective quotation, but these extracts will give some sense of how the writing works:

"But when at last we drove through the Dock," [Richard] continued, taken up by this urge to explain, "there was not one officer to report to, no-one to give orders, we simply drove on up a road towards what seemed to be our blaze . . ."

As he gave this inadequate description he was avidly living that moment again. It had been an unwilling ride.

(He was cold as they churned along in the taxi, which was boiling over from the distance it had been driven towing the heavy pump. Part of the steering wheel shone blood red from the sky. The air caught at his wind passage as though briars and their red roses were being dragged up from his lungs. The acrid air was warm, yet he was cold.)

But there was nothing in what he had spoken to catch her imagination. She went along at his side, by this path she hated, and looked up at his face in what he took to be the attention she was paying to the account he gave. . . .

"Excuse me a minute, darling," she said. "Christopher," she shouted, "come here. Do be careful. You'll only be getting wet through. That last lot of snow went all over you." . . .

"Look," his father interrupted, "haven't you knocked those branches about enough? There's hardly a bird left in the garden since you've been out. You'd do better to put food for them. They starve in this weather you know."

"They're Polish people," Christopher said, "and I'm a German policeman, rootling them about."[97]

Christopher's fantasy game is one of relatively few moments in the book when events outside England are mentioned. The firemen "hardly ever discussed the war," and when aspects of its progress in Europe are noted, it is with a terseness bordering on the offhand—at least until Dunkirk and the apparent likelihood that Britain will be invaded.[98] Pye, in particular, is so caught up with his professional and psychosexual muddles that he is "too disturbed to notice the invasion of Norway," and insofar as the war impinges on his thoughts, it is as a theater for social change. Characteristically, Green both satirizes Pye's class resentments and sympathizes with them. There's no mistaking the contrasts between

Pye and Roe, so claustrophobically entangled yet so utterly separated by determinants that not even war can change: luck, for example. So, Pye's tortured half-memories of an adolescent act of incest with his sister are set against the amiable tenderness between Richard and Dy; Pye is ditched by the girl with whom he has been having an affair, while Richard and Hilly have a more fulfilling, if temporary, relationship; and whereas the unmarried and childless Pye's kindness to a boy he finds in the street is fatally misinterpreted, Richard ends the book returning, complicatedly enough but far from unenviably, to his young son and the family home.

There is a half-submerged political theme, then, as well as a less schematic absorption in how these very different men resemble each other in both rebelling against and being subdued by the institutional relations, conventions, and perceptions of their working environment. The latter is one of the issues that the book carries forward from *Living;* and by a curious irony, *Caught* was itself modified by institutional pressures, to a degree unusual even in wartime.

There were various bowdlerizations, requested by the Hogarth Press on behalf of the printers, Garden City Press, which threatened that the Ministry of Labour, which controlled paper allocations, was inquiring about "the kind of work that was being printed when examining deferment requests etc."[99] John Lehmann protested but felt obliged to ask for cooperation from his increasingly irritated author, who reluctantly changed "I'm in the shit" to "I'm up the pole," "piss off" to "wee wee off," rephrased "I could manage more than those two in the same night" as ". . . in the same bed," and supplied a dozen other similarly coy tonings-down. The text seen by the printers early in 1943, however, had already been altered radically from the one that Green first submitted to Hogarth the previous autumn. The original typescript, with Green's handwritten alterations, still exists.[100] In it, Roe's wife is still alive. In this version, she is the woman named Dy, and she has most of the action and dialogue that in the published text is given to her sister, who doesn't appear at all. There are some passionate episodes between the couple, including one in which Roe worries that his wife will smell Hilly on his skin. All this was too much for the lawyer advising the Hogarth Press, Oswald Hickson, who feared that anyone who had worked with Henry and who resembled any of the main characters might have sued.[101] On Hickson's instructions, the book eventually included a preamble, declaring with more than usual implausibility that the characters are not drawn from life: Even Green had conceded that Mary Howells was partly based on an existing charwoman "whose daughter went mad."[102]

Apart from all this, everyone—Lehmann, Hickson, the printers, Leonard Woolf himself—felt a more general anxiety about the light in which the wartime fire service was being depicted.[103] In Woolf's view, the novel represented the fire station "as completely inefficient and corrupt from top to bottom without a single redeeming feature or even averagely competent and honest person in it." This opinion was partly supported by Stephen Spender, whom Lehmann asked to read the typescript. "It is too sour and bitter and gossipy, I think," Spender wrote, though he conceded that it was "genuine" and argued that no one who had actually experienced the Fire Service would find fault with it.

A consensus developed that one solution would be for the adultery to be removed: that what Green disarmingly called "Richards silly thing with Hilly" should just be dropped. Henry argued reasonably enough that adultery was "a frequent topic in novels."[104] He was known to be intransigent in his dealings with editors, and Lehmann worried that Green might take the book to another publisher. So it came as a surprise that the author seemed amenable to this seemingly fundamental objection. His way of dealing with it, though, was no less unexpected. Within a few weeks, he wrote back to Lehmann:

> Why should Richard Roe be married? Couldn't he be a widower? With a sister in law keeping house for him. This would make everything he now feels for his wife his feelings for his dead wife, which suits me better, in this book.
>
> Hickson was so upset about the adultery & there would be no adultery if Richard was a widower. Tell me what you think. Because I'm afraid Richards silly thing with Hilly is inevitable & essential to the makeup of the book.

Lehmann accepted the suggestion and did not have long to wait to see it implemented. Green made the necessary alterations with almost callous assurance and economy: a few cuts, a few rephrasings, and the wife (now nameless) is transformed—in a way perhaps influenced by Henry's own situation—into her sister. And whether it was by carelessness or design that the changes were left seemingly incomplete (Christopher calls his aunt "mummy," for example),[105] they give a new depth not only to *Caught*'s lugubrious mood but also to Richard's general air of bewilderment, drawing the book's bizarre incidents together into a phantasmagoria of grief. This is particularly true of the nightmarish, intensely visualized flashback to the kidnapping of Christopher, who in the published version represents Richard's, and the novel's, only real source of stability. But Richard's widowerhood also completes a no-less-symbolic strand of the book that laments the simultaneous compulsion and frailty of romantic love.

While *Caught* depicts some of the exhilaration of wartime sexual freedom, there is a tragic awareness both of what it half concealed and of what it could cost:

> these women seemed already given up to the male in uniform so soon to go away, these girls, as they felt, soon to be killed themselves, so little time left, moth deathly gay, in a daze of giving.
>
> That same afternoon the train to Portsmouth had wives dragged along the platform hanging limp to door handles and snatched off by porters in the way a man, standing aside, will pick bulrushes out of a harvest waggon load of oats.[106]

Roe's widowerhood fits this mood perfectly. If it helps make sense, too, of the lugubrious intensity of his behavior in the book, this may be because in the earlier version Henry had failed to translate into fiction the relationship between him and Dig's sister. Whatever the truth of that, he was sure that the censorship had brought about an improvement.[107]

CAUGHT EVENTUALLY APPEARED IN THE SUMMER OF 1943. By that time, the Blitz had effectively been reversed: Night after night, the RAF and USAF were dropping tens of thousands of tons of bombs on German industrial cities. Perhaps understandably, none of that impinged on reviews of the book. Philip Toynbee focused on the psychological intricacy of the narrative, with its "perpetual intrusion of the abnormal on the normal."[108] Margery Allingham saw it similarly as the story of Roe's "escape to the normal almost literally through fire."[109] Normality, for these critics, seems to have meant a country house with a young family in it, albeit one that no longer has a nanny to look after it. But as Elizabeth Bowen wrote, "writers are always slightly abnormal people: certainly, in so-called 'normal' times my sense of the abnormal has been very acute. In war, this feeling of slight differentiation was suspended. . . . Walls went down; and we felt, if not knew, each other. We all lived in a state of lucid abnormality." In practice, Bowen herself communicates that state less well than Henry Green, especially where other kinds of life are concerned: The working-class women in *The Heat of the Day* are music-hall caricatures by comparison with those in *Caught*. But "abnormality" in any case gets Green exactly wrong. It was his achievement to have conveyed, with all their discomfort and awkwardness and outright pain, the strange normalities in which, one way or another, people of all kinds, "rolled each in his or her own mystery," find themselves caught.

The title *Caught* alludes to fire, of course, but in the slang of the time the word could suggest romantic infatuation. Henry's love affairs were exhilarating, liberating—as Roe says in the novel, "anything is possible between people now"—but they were also dangerous. (Should we read anything into the fact that the fire station's sirens are misspelled *syrens* throughout the novel?) The affairs separated Henry from Dig without providing any alternative version of the security that he needed. *Caught* is full of loss, above all in its vision of Roe's dead wife, recalled with longing tenderness, much as the distant Dig was recalled by Henry: "now that he did not see her every evening, rather mocking, aloof, as gentle as he had been curt always, the touch of her white rose petal skin an unchanging part of what his life had been before."[110] The book is also permeated by a sense that things are going frighteningly out of control. Pye, whose managerial preoccupations partly figure Henry's own anxieties about Pontifex, lets the routine business of the station "run riot in his head" at night. Roe himself often feels thwarted, cut off socially from the other firemen and emotionally from Dy, with her "dislike of anything to do with the Service" and her resistance to the realities of his emotional experience. The book ends with a violent outburst by Richard against Dy, against women in general, and even—though he lamely tries to temper this—against his son:

> He let go. "God damn you," he shouted, releasing everything, "you get on my bloody nerves, all you bloody women with all your talk."
> It was as though he had gone for her with a hatchet. She went off without a word, rigid.
> He felt a fool at once and, in spite of it, that he had got away at last. Then his son came up, gravely looked at him.
> He said to Christopher, for the first time:
> "Get out," and he added,
> "Well, anyway, leave me alone till after tea, can't you?"

ONCE THE "BIG BLITZ" WAS OVER, DIG YORKE RE-turned to London. In 1942, the family left their house in Rutland Gate, which had been weakened structurally by the bombing, and took a lease on a much smaller establishment nearby, in Trevor Place. The change was influenced by financial considerations—taxes were high, and everyone knew that even when war ended things would still not be easy for the rich—but there seems to have been more than this behind the household's sudden contraction. Henry had been powerfully affected by his experiences in the Blitz, which had increased both his deafness and his tendencies to melancholy and paranoia. He was drinking more, both alone and in company. On Christmas Eve 1942, he wrote to Evelyn Waugh to congratulate him on *Put Out More Flags* and to thank him for the book's launch party. "How we came to part or how I came home I dont know," he wrote. "Am very depressed, lonely, & overworked."

CHAPTER 7

To Mary To Mary To Mary

THE NEW HOUSE, THOUGH IN THE SAME NEIGHBOR-hood as Rutland Gate, was, in Sebastian Yorke's later words, "miserably small" by the family's previous standards. You walked in from Trevor Place straight into a combined hall and dining room. Above this was a well-proportioned but diminutive L-shaped drawing room and, above that, two bedrooms. There was also a basement, occupied by the cook, who was now their only live-in servant. Harrods' redbrick warehouse dominated the foot of the street; Henry's local, the George IV, was just across from the front door, on the road leading into Montpelier Square. The terrace backed closely on houses facing Trevor Square, to the east.

Sebastian, who was to continue to spend large parts of his school holidays in the country with his grandparents, felt excluded by the move. "I suppose it was in a way rather nice for them," he acknowledges, "I mean it was all right just for a couple," but to him it seemed selfish of them.[1] From one point of view, of course, the scaling down was just an aspect of the social changes that are reflected in *Caught*, in which Richard Roe's parents move out of their big house into a lodge and Dy has no nanny. "The days of nurseries are over," Dy tells Richard, as she warns him that he'll be having tea with the children.[2] Outside the old nurseries, meanwhile, yet more extraordinary things were going on. American troops had arrived in England, and many of them were black. "I hear the most fascinating things about the negroes at Ashchurch," Henry wrote to Mary Strickland. "Tewkesbury will become a second

Harlem, with the most heavenly bands."[3] Some of his family and most of his old friends were living lives that would have been inconceivable to them a few years previously. Gerald, who had begun the war as a major in the Royal Gloucestershire Hussars, had been too old to go with the regiment to North Africa—where his and Henry's younger cousin Henry Wyndham was killed at El Alamein—and was moved to the Home Guard near Cambridge. Though Gerald was cheerful about his resulting demotion to the rank of captain-quartermaster, his wife found both it and Gerald's continuing scruffiness difficult to explain to her father, Major-General Sir John Duncan, who had had a brilliant military career and was now chief commissioner of the St. John Ambulance Brigade.[4]

Among Henry's friends, Harold Acton was a press censor, Brian Howard a clerk on a provincial RAF base, having been dismissed from MI5. Others were more substantially but not much more predictably occupied. Tony Powell was in the War Office, involved in military liaison with Britain's European allies and neutral powers. Goronwy Rees, now married, had been catapulted onto General Montgomery's staff and was based in a hotel in Somerset, helping to plan the invasion of France.[5] Evelyn Waugh was in London writing throughout most of 1942 and 1943, and Henry and Dig saw a lot of him there. But his active service in the commandos, especially in Crete, had added to the distance between him and some of his former friends. Behind Henry's back, he mocked what he saw as his boastful stories about the Fire Service. (Waugh's novel *Officers and Gentlemen* was to open with a wounding vignette in which a London club burns while "progressive novelists in firemen's uniform" ineffectually squirt "a little jet of water" into the drawing room.) Among others of their circle, Diana and Oswald Mosley had been imprisoned since 1940. One of the first letters that Diana Mosley received in jail was from the Yorkes.

A more painful letter of condolence had been needed in 1941, when Robert Byron was killed. With his firsthand knowledge of Austria and Germany, Byron had become an important influence in British counter-propaganda in the 1930s. He attended Nazi rallies with Diana Mosley's sister Unity Mitford, but his reaction to them could not have been more different from hers. He was among the first British observers who sympathetically grasped the full threat of Nazism to European Jewry. When war broke out, his intelligence connections and journalistic experience got him the job of reporting on Russian activities in Persia, but his ship had traveled no farther than the waters off the north of Scotland when it was torpedoed by the *Scharnhorst* in February 1941.[6]

Henry missed Robert very much—perhaps more than he knew. Robert had been among his closest male friends for more than twenty years: funny, supportive, intelligent, and unfailingly frank—one of the few who always said what he thought to Henry's face. In his last letter home, he had told his mother, "I regard this as a glorious war and am glad to be taking a more active part in it."[7] Henry's attitude was more equivocal, but he continued to play his role. The Fire Service was much less busy between the end of the Big Blitz in 1941 and the arrival of the first pilotless bombs, the V-1s, in 1944, so in July 1942 Henry was given leave in order to spend time at Pontifex. At first, there seemed little for him to do: "I sit in my swivel chair, swivelling and biting my nails just as I used to do."[8] But the firm had been getting involved in war work, as its technology was adaptable to the manufacture of two kinds of machine: ones that produced cordite, to kill people, and ones that made penicillin, to help heal those the cordite did not manage to kill. Russia badly needed both materials. Henry's earlier contacts in Moscow now bore fruit in the form of orders worth half a million pounds.[9] In the summer of 1943, he told Rosamond Lehmann that he was working so hard that he had been forced to cut down his drinking almost to nothing, though he confessed that he still made "a feeble pass at the youngest girls, like an old fool of 80."[10]

The latest of these girls was the very tall, aloof-seeming, turbulent, and staggeringly beautiful Mary Keene, who had met Henry and Dig through Augustus John's daughter, Poppet. Mary was brought up in the East End of London; her father died in an institution after being disabled in an electrical accident at work, and her mother was volatile, neglectful, and sometimes violent. Mary herself had lost her right foot when she had been knocked down by a truck at the age of nine and had spent some of her childhood as a boarder at a "cripple school." She ran away from home when she was about sixteen and worked in sewing shops on Commercial Road. Then a man who had picked her up introduced her to Cedric Morris's art school at Dedham, in Essex, where Lucian Freud was among the students. Now twenty-one, unhappily married to the forty-year-old filmmaker and former art dealer Ralph ("Bunny") Keene, she was befriended by a painter who was also important in Henry's life: Matthew Smith. Both Matthew and Mary represented a significant trend in his new relationships, away from people of his own social background and toward those who were less categorizable, more "bohemian," often less stable.

Like Henry, Matthew had been set on the life of an artist from an early age and in defiance of his background.[11] His father, a rich but strict northern manufacturer, had put him into a woolen mill in Bradford, where he became besotted by the colors of the dyes. The young man insisted on going to art school in Manchester, where his father tried to deflect him into industrial design and supposed he could forbid him to attend any class that involved undressed women. By 1914, within ten years of leaving Manchester, Smith had been to the Slade School, had married an artist named Gwen Salmond, and had exhibited at the Salon des Indépendants.

One of his first good paintings depicts a thin, anxious-looking, bespectacled man of indeterminate age, buttoned-up, tie knotted neatly, hat pressed down firmly. It is a self-portrait painted in 1909, and this is how the artist went on looking and dressing for the next fifty years. Journalists and others who did not know him well naturally assumed that the appearance indicated the existence of "two Mr. Smiths," the clerkly puritan and the painter. The truth is both simpler and much more complex and resembles at least one truth about Henry Yorke. There was in fact only one Matthew Smith: a nervous man in love with beauty and especially with women, on whom he depended, most of whom could not depend on him, and some of whom he cost in terms of their own art.

At the beginning of the war, Smith's sons had joined the RAF. By the end of 1941, both had been killed. The artist was incapacitated by grief and spent several desperate months trailing alone around London from one lodging house to another, unable to settle or to do any work. At last, after various attempts, he found a rural idyll of his own in a rented Tudor house at Stratford Saint Mary, near Dedham. Mary Keene, whom he met around the time of his second son's death, helped to revive his imaginative strength and purpose, and his portraits of this time and later have a new psychological sharpness, not least about Mary herself, whom he showed not only as a statuesque goddess but more interestingly as a brooding, introspective figure, her slanting gray eyes resistantly averted from him.

Mary was trouble: It is the word everyone uses of her. But it was the kind of trouble that stirred men's imagination and drew out an apprehensive kind of tenderness in them. At one time she was involved with Louis MacNeice, who she believed described her in his poem "The Kingdom":[12]

> *Too large in feature for a world of cuties,*
> *Too sculptured for a cocktail lounge flirtation,*
> *This girl is almost awkward, carrying off*
> *The lintel of convention on her shoulders,*
> *A Doric river-goddess with a pitcher*
> *Of ice-cold wild emotions. Pour them where she will*
> *The pitcher will not empty. . . .*
>   *. . . Vitality and fear*
> *Are marbled in her eyes, from hour to hour*
> *She changes like the sky—one moment is so gay*
> *That all her words are laughter but the next*
> *Moment she is puzzled, her own Sphinx,*
> *Made granite by her destiny. . . .*

Henry's affair with Mary had begun while he was laboriously rewriting *Caught*. Almost immediately, he began thinking about his next novel. Though his first outline of the plot and characters is titled "Service," Henry knew by the end of 1943 that the book's title would be *Loving*.[13]

One weekend in February 1943, when Mary and Henry were already lovers, she took him to stay with Matthew Smith at Stratford Saint Mary.[14] Henry felt as refreshed there "as a donkey that has been allowed to drop its burden," or so he wrote afterward. He attributed the feeling to his release from alternately scrubbing fire-station floors and overseeing the production of cordite plants at Pontifex, but it is clear that circumstances in general were combining to make him feel more relaxed and confident than he had for some time. The successes of Pontifex, however temporary they were to prove, were a coup not only in them-

The Ledbury Hunt meet at Forthampton Court. Vincent Yorke on horseback and his foxhounds are in the foreground.

Henry Yorke, age one and three quarters, with his brothers Philip (left) and Gerald.

Left: *Henry, "plump, uncompetitive, and nervous," in 1910.* Right: *Henry at about age fifteen. His school friend Anthony Powell remembered him as "an unremitting talker . . . hit or miss . . . but . . . funny, perceptive, highly individual."*

Henry and Dig at a family party in August 1928, while Henry was working in Birmingham.

*Henry and Dig's wedding, July 1929. "Buying a top hat is absolutely hellish,"
Henry told Ottoline Morrell. On the day itself, which was hot and dry, his cautious umbrella caused comment.* FROM THE COLLECTION OF JOHN YORKE

Henry's brother Gerald and his wife, Angela, flanked by Maud and Vincent Yorke, ca. 1937. Angela won Henry's respect by always kissing the forbidding Vincent good-night. FROM THE COLLECTION OF JOHN YORKE

Party going: Diana Guinness (soon to be Mosley) and John Sutro at a fancy-dress party of the latter's at the Savoy, 1932. Henry and Dig were there. FROM THE COLLECTION OF LADY DIANA MOSLEY

Rosamond Lehmann.

John Lehmann. FROM THE
COLLECTION OF HULTON GETTY

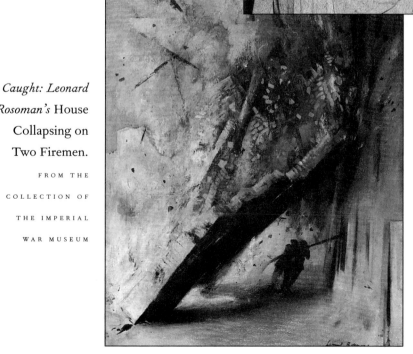

*Caught: Leonard
Rosoman's* House
Collapsing on
Two Firemen.
FROM THE
COLLECTION OF
THE IMPERIAL
WAR MUSEUM

Kitty Freud in 1951. FROM THE
COLLECTION OF KITTY GODLEY

*Mary Keene in the 1940s. Louis
MacNeice may have been thinking of
her when he wrote: "This girl is
almost awkward, carrying off /
The lintel of convention on her
shoulders . . . Vitality and fear /
Are marbled in her eyes, from hour
to hour / She changes like the sky."*
FROM THE COLLECTION OF

ALICE KEENE

Portrait of Henry Green, II. *By Matthew Smith, copyright © 1948.*

Henry with Terry and Carol Southern and "Pussle."

selves but also in his dealings with his father, who had resisted Henry's chemical plant–manufacturing venture. However illusory his financial anxieties had been, the move to Trevor Place alleviated them. Above all, Mary herself had a unique combination of qualities that Henry needed and to which he temporarily abandoned himself, inscribing a copy of one of his books "To Mary To Mary To Mary."[15] She was affectionate, reckless, and physically very attractive; she loved art and aspired to it; though unintellectual, she was intensely intuitive, in the same kind of half-oblivious way as Henry himself; and she was classless. Even Dig loved her, though her affection was badly repaid. By October 1943, Mary was pregnant. There was some question about whether the father was Henry; such doubts were to enter the torments of the central character in his next novel, *Back*. Whatever the truth of the matter, Henry gave Mary financial help in her divorce from Bunny in 1946.

The relationship was never smooth. In one of her undated letters to Matthew, Mary says she has "a great hangover, and a huge grazed bruise on my forehead and a little black eye all because of a great dramatic meeting with beloved Henry. It was so madly gay."[16] Accused of stealing some nightgowns from a friend, Mary took violent offense when Henry mischievously suggested that she might enjoy reading *Moll Flanders*.[17] She found Dig "miserable," as she well might have been, "very cross and suspicious," and sometimes felt sorry for her, telling Matthew that he was wrong to think that all was well between her and Henry. But Mary admitted that she felt spiteful toward the older woman, too, and that she sometimes goaded her, for example by showing her an expensive new dress, implying that Henry had bought it for her.[18]

Years later, Mary wrote an autobiographical novel, published posthumously under the title *Mrs. Donald*.[19] (When she was small, her mother had married a marine engineer named MacDonald.) Written in a style much influenced by Henry Green's, the book is primarily a version of Mary's impoverished, violent childhood, told as the story of three women, Mrs. Donald herself and her daughters, Rose and Violet. Violet is abused by her brother and finally runs away from home. This thread of the narrative is intercut with episodes from her later affair with a poet-painter named Louis who is a composite of Louis MacNeice, Matthew Smith, and—predominantly—Henry Yorke. The predicament of the mistress, who has been introduced to Louis by his complaisant wife, Di, is evoked beautifully and passionately, especially in how she has to live entirely in the present, cut off from her background, so that she is agonizingly and unpreparedly "responsible for herself."[20]

Louis is presented as responsible to nothing except to his art. His response to other aspects of life is a mixture of fear and passivity. When he first falls in love with and marries Di, it is because she represents "progress to freedom, an escape from his father."[21] Di is strong, socially grand, and a shade manipulative, but she conceals her strength behind an elegance that surrounds her "like a dimension."[22] Part of this elegance lies in avoiding anything too explicit: The more powerful a necessity is, the more she treats it as unmentionable.[23] She is also, Violet senses, very lonely, in a way that communicates itself as "famine in the room," a famine that Violet inevitably feels unable to relieve.

The scale of the needs that Violet imputes to Di and Louis may, of course, say more about herself than about them. This is an important caveat, not only because the fiction treats Di as an active partner in Violet's affair with Louis but also because it imputes to Louis a determination to get Violet pregnant:

> He longed to start something inside her so that she would accept him as a man. Through his child she would love him—Him! At the thought of himself he almost wept. He saw himself in this image as if tucked away, a blind spore inside her that must come to birth.[24]

This does not sound much like Henry, though Louis and he have other traits in common, including more attractive ones like their taste for gossip and anecdote.[25] But Mary also told her daughter something that, while still exaggerated, suggests a trait both more convincing and more revealing about Henry Yorke. "He didn't really exist," she said. "There was a hole there. He only really existed in other people. He was living off the fat of other people and once the fat had gone, he would go." These are vengeful words, but they correspond to what others noticed.[26]

Whatever Mary's later view of Henry's attitude, his initial reaction to her pregnancy seems to have been one of little more than surprise and confusion, combined with fear that, far from tying her to him, the baby would take her away.[27] He wrote her a hurried, garbled outpouring of platitudes, saying that he hoped the child—her first—would "cement everything into a sort of keep" that would protect her from unhappiness. She was too honest for ordinary life, he suggested, and this caused her to be hurt by other people's dishonesty, so she might find consolation in the honesty of a child. Anyway, children "are the perpetuation of life & therefore . . . sacred when they are small." He hoped that she would never regret having it. He added, "Being yours I shall love it & I only hope it will not make any fundamental difference."

It couldn't not have made a difference, of course. Alice was born on 14 May 1944. At the height of Mary's affair with Henry, there had been periods when the two were together every night.[28] Already, things had changed—not only because of Mary's involvement with Alice but as a result of the new danger faced by everyone in the south of England from flying bombs. As soon as she could, Mary took the baby to Wales, where they lived with her friends Dylan and Caitlin Thomas.

In some ways, her move came as a relief to Henry. The affair had developed just when, with Dig's return to London, his marriage had seemed likely to revive. What had previously always involved an element of light fantasy—Henry and Mary once sent a telegram to Matthew Smith pretending that they were celebrating the liberation of France by going to Aix-en-Provence together[29]—was now all too pressingly real. He reminded her, perhaps also as a way of reminding himself, that he was not a free, bohemian artist but a semirespectable married business-man with a young son and a cat. Only a month before the birth, Henry wrote to Mary from Forthampton, with affection yet also with a far from tactful insistence on the actualities of his separate—and rich—domestic existence (even in 1944 there were ham and eggs on his parents' sideboard). Still, he was finding it very painful to let go of her, and the signals given out by the letter are deeply equivocal. He begins "Darling, darling, darling" and describes a conversation with the ten-year-old Sebastian about women, into which he had introduced Mary as a topic, as if Sebastian were a friend he was talking to in the pub. "I asked him if he thought you were beautiful. He said he thought your face was. I said what about the rest of you. He replied, 'I think her body's too thin. . . .' So now you know, darling, now you know."[30]

As if these complications weren't enough, Henry was still juggling other relationships, past and present. In 1943, the Hogarth Press's list of people to whom free copies of his books should be sent had included not only Dig, her sister Mary Lowry-Corry, and Mary Keene, but also Rosemary Clifford, Ann Glass, Lady Diana Worthington, a Mrs. Bergne, and Pauline Gates. Pauline's daughter Venetia believes that of these, the most dangerous to Henry's marriage was Miss, though if so, the danger may have been stronger in Henry's mind than in hers: According to her daughter, Miss "always loved Henry but Goronwy Rees was the love of her life."[31] But Gates caused shock waves of her own. Sometime in 1944 or 1945, when Gates's relationship with her second husband was at a low ebb, the Yorkes gave refuge to the twelve- or thirteen-year-old Venetia in Sebastian's room while he was away at school.[32] Venetia, whose father had been killed while reporting the Spanish civil war from the Republican side,[33] became very close to the couple and over the years was to observe their marriage with the closeness of a clever adolescent, at first hand as well as through what her never discreet mother told her. Like others who knew Dig well, Venetia both admired and was perturbed by her capacity to pretend—perhaps even to believe—that anything unpleasant in life just wasn't happening, concealing behind a manner of "the most brilliant feyness" not only what she knew but whether she knew it at all. (In later years, this self-protective code, too deep to be called a veneer, too conventional for a psychosis, made a new Japanese friend of the couple feel uncomfortably close to home.)[34] Whatever Dig's underlying unhappiness and however far down it may have been buried, Venetia is sure that it was perfectly clear both to Dig and to Henry's girlfriends that he "would never in a million years get divorced from her or leave her." Henry was unfailingly courteous to Dig, and "the whole thing was totally eighteenth century." As for his behavior with Pauline, though she loved making violent rows there was never one with Henry. "He must have had terrific character, that man," said Venetia. "He managed to stop all these really rather high-octane ladies from throwing the crockery at him." In due course, the affair settled down into a friendship, assignations at the Orchid Room and the Gargoyle gradually ceding to harmless dog races at White City while the two couples continued to have lunch and dinner in each other's houses.

Rosamond Lehmann, meanwhile, was finally divorcing Wogan Philipps after their long separation and was on the last lap of her own new novel, *The Ballad and the Source*.[35] She received her copy of *Caught* through her brother and wrote to Henry about it with excited enthusiasm as well as with considerable critical acuity. He replied to her strictures immediately and in detail, admitting, for example, that he was prone to inconsistencies and implausibilities but stressing the importance he put on overall composition and construction, in a painterly rather than intellectual sense of the word:

> I hadn't until I opened your letter realised that Christopher was shown alone in the store. That's a mistake. As to the store episode, it is meant to echo in Pye's final scene & to counterbalance the colour in the dock burning. In particular to be literary while the dock is actual, thus to give Richard depth in showing him growing up. But I did not let this plan work out in detail or completely, as I was afraid it might confuse the reader, & compromised by leaving it as a counterbalance at both ends of the see saw.

He wrote for only about six people, he told Rosamond, and she was one of them; her approval justified everything.[36]

Whether or not those for whom the book was written included his relations, they had mixed feelings about it. The more conservative of them deplored its presentation of the less reputable aspects of London under the Blitz. The more lighthearted, especially Henry's cousins Ursula and Mark Wyndham and their mother, Gladys, speculated hilariously among themselves on the plausibility of the incident in which "a man . . . had sexual intercourse with his sister, under the misapprehension that she was an entirely different woman."[37] Mark, who was in the army in the Middle East, opined with military firmness that "*no* night is so dark one could not recognise someone at a range of zero, unless of course he kept his eyes shut through the whole business" but reserved final judgment pending further discussion with Ursula "and Daddy and John and Aunt Midge."

In the midst of all this private discussion, *Caught* was widely and for the most part favorably reviewed, and it sold well.[38] In the *New Statesman,* where it was aptly paired for review with Graham Greene's *The Ministry of Fear,* Philip Toynbee described his exhilaration at encountering "two proper novelists, bravely immune to the general decay."[39] Henry Green, he said, had "converted observed fact into imagined truth," achieving an intimate play between routine and fantasy. His working-class characters were free from "all music-hall conceptions" and also from "the heavy heroics of so-called 'proletarian' writing." In *Time and Tide,* the novelist Margery Allingham—the only critic who saw that the book's intensity derives in part from the experiences through which Richard Roe has passed[40]—also praised its freedom from propaganda, contrasting it with another new novel, J. B. Priestley's *Daylight on Saturday,* which is set in an aircraft factory and in which, by contrast, she found "a little too much of Mr Priestley priesting."

The fact that *Caught* is unflattering to the British war effort caused Green some nervousness when a request came to Hogarth for permission to translate it into German. The dilemma had become a familiar one, to visual artists as well as to writers. Which was better? To be able to show that the arts in Britain were untrammeled by censorship—and, partly for that reason, imaginative and original, if not particularly positive in outlook—or to present a more optimistic, if artistically unexciting, picture of what was going on? The British Council took the first view and encouraged a project to translate *Caught* into Italian so that it could be made available in territory newly occupied by the Allies.[41] As far as the German proposal was concerned, Henry was worried about "whether our allowing a . . . translation is to invite Goebbels to make use of the book. . . . I cant think of anything worse than to have people saying 'that's the man whose books were used for German propaganda in the last war.' "[42] He finally allowed himself to be persuaded that it would be read only in German-speaking areas of neutral Switzerland.

One way and another, he was in an unsteady frame of mind. *Penguin New Writing* had recently published a long piece about *Caught* containing some hints of criticism, which Henry took very badly. It was part of a regular series, "A Reader's Notebook," written by "Jack Marlowe" and ambiguously poised between an editorial and a more personal point of view.[43] The piece compared *Caught* with C. S. Forester's new book, *The Ship:* the story of a light cruiser involved in protecting a convoy on its way through the Mediterranean to Malta. A novel of this kind, "Marlowe" argues, "performs a real service in wartime" even though it "misses being an imaginative work of the first order." *Caught,* by contrast, "would not make anyone think the better of the British war-effort. . . . One feels like protesting that though human beings may be like this, they are also moved by warm and generous emotions." Still, the author conceded that while the novel does not propagandize in the con-ventional sense, "it *is* propaganda—for the vitality of imaginative litera-ture in England under the most difficult conditions." If not all of Green's stylistic experiments work, he wrote, the dialogue is uniquely vital and truthful in a way that exposes its speakers "with an icy precision that one would call merciless if it were not extremely funny."

The essay moved on, via Maurice Bowra's new book, *The Heritage of Symbolism,* to questions about the social role of the artist and the de-fense of imaginative freedom. There was still a place for poetry in the modern world, Bowra had written, "because it does something that nothing else can do." This was an important thing to say, and there was a special aptness in the juxtaposition of Bowra's words with a discussion of his old friend's new novel. But all Henry noticed on first reading the piece was its few words of criticism. In a mood that he described later as "unreasoning savagery,"[44] he fired off a complaint to John Lehmann saying that "Jack Marlowe" was "no good" and was "just turning the words out for money."[45]

What rankled, apart from a suggestion that *Caught* fell short of being a masterpiece, was the criticism of what he had been particularly anxious to get right: the real behavior of the firemen. He was particularly worried that he had made a wrong decision about the German transla-tion and was mortified when Sylvester Gates attacked him for it at a din-ner party in January 1944. Gates's view was that the book would obviously be bought in Germany and that whatever its effects, this con-stituted trading with the enemy: strong words from one businessman to another.[46]

All the same, Green pressed on with his current book, which was set in Ireland—a neutral country where he had seen happier times. By De-cember 1943, he had already drafted twenty-five thousand words,[47] and as early as the following March a version was being read by Matthew Smith, who, Henry told Mary, made "a great song & dance about it."[48] Henry revised it throughout the summer of 1944 and delivered the type-script in October. John Lehmann told Rosamond that it was "another masterpiece."[49]

LOVING, AS HAS OFTEN BEEN POINTED OUT, IS CAST in the form of an ironic fairy tale. It begins "Once upon a day" and ends "they were married and lived happily ever after." But beneath the romantic-seeming surface of life in a castle in neutral Ireland, Green, like Chekhov and Turgenev, depicts the mutually dependent operations— economic, sexual, "political" in the broadest sense—of an entire feudal household, from the frivolous, oblivious chatelaine Mrs. Tennant and her daughter-in-law, Violet, who is having an affair with a neighbor, Captain Davenport, to the English servants who are the main characters: the overpromoted new butler, Charley Raunce, the nanny, cook, house-maids (including Raunce's much younger girlfriend, Edith), and beyond them a symbolically incomprehensible Irish lampman, Paddy O'Conor.[50] There isn't a party line in this: The world described is absurd and unsat-isfactory, yet it is beautiful at the same time, and there is no sense that another world would be preferable. At the end, when Raunce and Edith run away home to England, Raunce is ill, they are going to live under the nose of his mother, a possessive bully, Edith is likely to be called up for war work, and they are abandoning the part-filched comforts of Kinalty Castle for rationing and bombs. One of the reasons for Raunce's illness is his anxiety about having fiddled his employers' housekeeping accounts. Both the antihero and the situation are reminiscent, then, of aspects of *Living* as well as of *Caught*. No less typical, but newly assured, is the bit-tersweet mixture of tones:

> Edith laid her lovely head on Raunce's nearest shoulder and above them, above the great shadows laid by trees those white birds wheeled in a sky of eggshell blue and pink with a remote sound of applause as, circling, they clapped their stretched, starched wings in flight.
>
> That side of Edith's face open to the reflection of the sky was a deep red.
>
> "She passed my books all right this mornin'," he murmured.
>
> "What books?" she asked low and sleepy.
>
> "Me monthly accounts," he replied.

"Did she?" Edith sighed content. . . .
"You're wonderful," she said so low he hardly heard.

As usual, it is hard to catch the tonal complexities of the quotation out of context, and any summary of the story is inadequate in different ways. The plot goes like this: Mrs. Tennant, a widow, is left in charge of Kinalty Castle because her son, Jack, is away at the war. Her problems are worsened by the death of her old butler, Eldon, and by the various tensions that arise among the servants both when the footman, Charley Raunce, is given his place and when—though Mrs. Tennant never learns this—one of the maids finds Dermot Davenport in bed with Mrs. Tennant's daughter-in-law, Violet. The ancient nanny, meanwhile, is ill, so the servants have extra work to do looking after not only Violet and Jack's two small daughters but a new arrival in the form of a cockney boy named Albert, who is either the cook's nephew or her illegitimate son and who has been brought to the safety of Kinalty as a favor to her. Deprived of the authority of Jack Tennant and the old butler, and against a background of fear of Germany and the IRA and guilt at being in a neutral country while the mainland is being bombed, the household gradually yields to misrule. Between lavish meals and furtive nips at whatever quantities of drink can be slipped through the various accounts books, Raunce flirts with Edith; Kate, the other housemaid, flirts with Paddy; Violet carries on her affair with Dermot Davenport; Mrs. Tennant loses a sapphire ring; and young Albert brings his own miniature version of wartime chaos, throttling one of the peacocks, which Paddy is responsible for, and introducing the young Tennant girls to a new vocabulary of swearwords.

In all this, Jack Tennant is allowed some leave, and his wife and mother go to England to join him, with Captain Davenport in hot pursuit. Left to their own devices at Kinalty, the servants have some innocent fun, the cook taking to the gin bottle, the housemaids dancing in the ballroom and playing blindman's buff with the pantryboy, Raunce and Edith making themselves comfortable in front of the library fire. Raunce introduces a more serious level of anarchy, however, scaring himself and the other servants with talk of the IRA and, when Edith finds Mrs. Tennant's ring, suggesting in a muddled, oblique access of transferred guilt that she hide it again in case she is thought to have taken it in the first place. Edith tells one of the children where it is hidden, it disappears once more, and the ensuing panic and attempts at cover-up reach the first of a number of farcical climaxes when an insurance agent arrives and the servants' stories fail to match. Raunce and Edith now reach a decision to get married, and Albert the pantryboy, whether in a jealous pique or incensed at falling under suspicion of stealing the ring or both, announces that he is going to leave Kinalty and enlist as an air-force gunner. The swings of mood become still more extreme after the Tennants return: Mrs. Tennant is exasperated by not being able to get to the bottom of what has happened to her ring, even after it is returned to her; this, to her, rightly symbolizes her lack of control over her whole household. Furthermore, Violet is in a turmoil of guilt and divided affection between Jack and Dermot; the nanny is dying; the cook throws a drunken tantrum; and Raunce understandably gives way under the pressure, aware that he can't hold down his situation and worried about the fact that he is twice the age of the beautiful, flirtatious, impulsive Edith, who nonetheless seems eager to marry him. At the end, the couple runs away to England.

Green liked to tell how he had taken a cue for his masterpiece from one of the former domestic servants with whom he worked in the Fire Service, "who told me that when he was second footman in a large place the then butler had said to him: 'What I enjoy most, Favell, is to lie in bed on a Sunday morning with the windows open, listening to the church bells, eating buttered toast with cunty fingers.' "[51] The anecdote distills the novel's sense of truancy, opportunism, and irresponsibility, feelings that Henry Yorke himself was both enjoying and feeling guilty about at the time he was writing it. Evelyn Waugh may have been making a personal point at his expense when he criticized the book's "nymphomania."[52] There are many parallels to Henry's situation, perhaps not least when Violet is startled into a moment's thought about her absent husband and resolves, briefly and ambivalently, to stop seeing Davenport. Raunce, too, his intense if blundering amativeness matched by his anxieties, is in part a reflection of his author, and in him the book's depiction of sexuality is linked with a still more complex theme of social responsibility.

Green not only understands, with P. G. Wodehouse, the power of someone in Raunce's position but uniquely conveys his vulnerability. Raunce is dependent on the Tennant family, who may prove as impermanent as their name implies. Very early in the book, Mrs. Tennant mentions her worries about taxation. One of the reasons why, in the end, Raunce takes Edith home to England is his fear that "the way things are shapin' it wouldn't come as a surprise if places such as this weren't doomed to a natural death."[53] It was a common fear, of course, that war and high taxation would bring the end of the great country house—fears that were to prove justified both in Dig's family, whose Ledbury mansion was sold after the war, and at Petworth, which was handed over to the National Trust. As Evelyn Waugh later wrote, it looked as though "the ancestral seats which were our chief national artistic achievement were doomed to decay and spoliation like the monasteries in the sixteenth century." If this was felt in England, how much more so in Anglo-Ireland, with the older threat of Irish Republicanism added to what the widely feared German invasion might have done. The novel is oblique about this, as Green's work is about everything. His characters' fears come and go like the weather, and the only apocalyptic hint in the narrative (rather than in people's talk) is ambiguous: The Blue Drawing Room at Kinalty, we are told, was "the most celebrated eighteenth-century folly in Eire that had still to be burned down."[54] Whether it in fact *will* be burned down or whether the Tennants will sell it and leave is less clear than how comically at odds the present relationships are among the castle, its inhabitants, and their surroundings.

Brideshead Revisited, Evelyn Waugh's novel of the same year, and not the irreverent and unsnobbish *Loving,* set the tone for the postwar religion of "heritage"—though that has a long literary ancestry, not least in Ireland. Rod Mengham has interestingly pointed out that Yeats's poem "Ancestral Houses"—the first of his "Meditations in Time of Civil War"—anticipates some of Henry Green's themes, particularly the idea that great architecture, by remembering the powers and ambitions of those who paid for it, casts an ironic light on their heirs:

> *But when the master's buried, mice can play,*
> *And maybe the great-grandson of that house,*
> *For all its bronze and marble, 's but a mouse.*

To Green, such ironies suggested a satirical fantasy, the humor of which would have been beyond Yeats.

Everything at Kinalty is in danger of collapsing, a result, in part, of the castle's intrinsic preposterousness. Even its dovecote is modeled on the leaning tower of Pisa. Such a tower looks likely to fall, and related jokes are found in other parts of the house that architecturally mimic social revolution. By a Marie Antoinettish conceit, for example, a cowshed has been promoted into the extravagance of the Blue Drawing Room. Here sits Mrs. Tennant on a gothic hammock, "surrounded by milking stools, pails, clogs, the cow byre furniture all in gilded wood." There could be no better setting for her incomprehension of any world beyond herself, whether that of her adulterous daughter-in-law ("your contemporaries have all got this amazing control of yourselves. . . . Violet dear I think you are perfectly wonderful and Jack's a very lucky man") or of her staff:

> "My dear it's not for us to understand O'Conor," Mrs. Tennant explained as she replaced into its niche a fly-whisk carved out of a block of sandalwood, the handle enamelled with a reddish silver. "We don't have to live with the servants. Not yet . . ."

In the society of *Loving*, such negligence affects everyone. In real life, Henry and Dig were not good with domestic staff, yet the novel shows with an unfaltering clarity—severity even—how the servants' failings reflect and emphasize those of their "superiors" and of the social structure in which they are all occupied.[55] Mrs. Tennant's carelessness with her jewelry is the most obvious example, with the all-pervasive suspicion, cupidity, deception, and panic that it brings to Kinalty. Her complacency is mirrored in—has perhaps influenced—the old nanny's refusal to hear anything bad about the family. It encouraged the financial corruption of the late butler, Eldon, which is so quickly picked up by his successor. It finds an echo, too, in the anti-Irishness of most of the household.

Their chauvinism—"We're really in enemy country here you know," Mrs. Tennant tells Raunce by way of excusing the fact that his new duties won't bring him more pay[56]—dramatizes the national divisions that Henry and Dig had encountered on holidays in Ireland, not least as guests of the earl of Rosse at his eighteenth-century gothic seat, Birr Castle in County Offaly. The Irish now like to claim Birr as the original of Kinalty in *Loving*, though the mansions have few details in common. Kinalty is a composite: Green took some details from Birr but others from a range of other houses. The bucolic extravagance of its drawing room probably derives from the one at Hamels, in Hertfordshire, designed by John Soane for Henry's eighteenth-century ancestor the third earl of Hardwicke; the topographical overmantel perhaps from Howth Castle in County Dublin; the star-painted ceiling from descriptions of the Great Chamber at Theobalds, in Hertfordshire; the dovecote from fantasy.[57] Kinalty, like Shakespeare's Illyria, is both nowhere and everywhere.

As we have seen, the novel encodes powerful experiences of Henry's at this time. The tussle between the romantic moments of his affair with Mary Keene and its more restricted actualities finds expression in a complex set of fictional symbols: the freedom of birds in an often destructive environment; maids waltzing in a dust-sheeted ballroom. Such episodes or epiphanies in the book have a pure element of what Yeats, in "Ancestral Houses," called "life's own self-delight"; but they are also loaded with ironic meaning. In their game of blindman's buff, the servants use a scarf that was given to Edith by Violet (who was given it by whom?) and is decorated with the words "I love you I love you."[58] Love, then, or so this beautiful and delicate metaphor implies, can both be given and given away, put on and cast off. It is also blinding, dizzying, a confuser of identity. Yet in the game, no one identifies anyone wrongly. Once again, Green uses names to convey an unusual range of meanings. Raunce's boy, Albert, gets his guess right, but some of the more serious confusions around him arise through the presence of two Alberts at Kinalty, himself and the cook's nephew. ("One name less for Mrs. T. to remember.")[59] Even Charley Raunce can't be quite sure who he is, for he has only recently been promoted from head footman, and this household adheres to the old custom of calling all footmen by the same name, to save trouble: "all the Toms, Harrys, Percys, Victors one after the other, all called Arthur."[60] Mrs. Tennant's way of letting him know she has promoted him is to say, "Very well then . . . I suppose we shall have to call you Raunce."[61] He thanks her, but the change is short-lived: "We know we can rely on you you know Arthur," she confides, a slip that she continues to make almost until the end of the book.[62]

If questions about the rigidity of class barriers continued to nag at Henry's imagination, they may have been exacerbated by his affair with Mary: probably the point farthest from his and Dig's world to which his relationships had ever taken him. And her pregnancy seems to have prompted another of the themes running beneath *Loving*: absent or negligent or otherwise dubious fathers. Jack Tennant, whose own father is dead, is mainly away at war. The brief part of his leave that he passes in Ireland is spent fishing: He shows no interest in his daughters. He is offhand about, even oblivious to, Violet's relationship with Davenport, though Tennant's daughter, Moira, has noticed it enough to dislike it, and there is more than a hint that Violet may be pregnant by him.[63] The other child in the novel, the evacuee Albert, seems to be fatherless, and we learn that the fathers of both the other Albert and Raunce are dead.[64] In fact, the only paternal relationship in the book is a parody of one: that of Raunce—like his author, forty years old—with his young girlfriend. "Come and sit by father," Raunce likes to say to her.[65]

If there was any paternalism in Henry's relationships with younger women, there isn't much sign of it in the letters that he and Mary wrote to each other when she was living with Dylan and Caitlin Thomas. Henry's mainly consist of extravagantly black, half-comic anecdotes about his daily life and about mutual friends. A woman named Natalie has been crippled "again" by Bob—a jealous husband, it seems—while another woman has been overheard plotting to attack her with a stick for the fourth time.[66] One of the staff of Pontifex, a man of fifty-eight, has come into his office and cried like a child.[67] The Yorkes have been to Brighton, but Henry's enjoyment of the Bedford Hotel has been spoiled by the fact that one of the waiters was also named Henry and a woman guest called him "all day long with a quavering cry & I got persecution mania."[68]

Mary, meanwhile, had more concrete reasons for feeling persecuted. The Thomases were renting a bungalow in New Quay, Cardiganshire, where the poet's friendship with the wife of a commando captain provoked a drunken fight. The soldier came home on leave armed with a machine gun, went to the bungalow where Mary and Caitlin were looking after their young children, and fired a dozen rounds into the flimsy asbestos walls before bursting in with a grenade.[69] The episode and its legal aftermath formed a sensational backdrop to Mary's split with Bunny Keene and gave undeniable urgency to her concerns about where she should live and on what. She now described New Quay as an "open air loony bin" of which "I'll have no pleasant recollections . . . instead I shall shudder & groan." She impressed a shy local policeman by saying that her stay there was worse than anything she had experienced in the Blitz.

As far as money was concerned, Henry for the moment seemed expansive: "You will never be in real need so long as Mathew [*sic*] & I are alive as you know & little Alice must always be on a bed of roses."[70] Accommodation was more of a problem. He quickly made clear that Trevor Place was "out of the question." She wondered whether Augustus John might be able to house her in Chelsea, but Henry fended off this idea, too, suggesting—to Mary's understandable irritation—that a pub in Wales might still be the best solution.[71] He bemoaned feeling separated from her "by these wild Welsh mountains,"[72] but there were other forms of separation between them, as he continually found ways of reminding her. In an odd echo of the plot of *Loving,* some jewelry of Dig's was stolen around this time. When the insurance came through, Henry wrote to Mary telling her that they had spent an hour at Cartier's, which was preparing a "scheme" for some new pieces for Dig. She "will be literally brilliant with diamonds quite soon," he joked tactlessly.[73]

Meanwhile, he took satisfaction in Mary's disenchantment with Dylan Thomas, whom she had described to him as "an extraordinary abnormal person, . . . the most uncivilised I've known." He had already warned Mary that the poet's behavior was "a form of inverted snobbery at its most odious. Exactly like the *Tatler* only the other way round" and was content to have his reservations confirmed.[74] Matthew Smith eventually found Mary a place in Chelsea, though she continued to stay with the Thomases until June 1945, keeping well away from Bunny while the lawyers were busy with their separation.

Henry was paying her legal costs: a painful outlay for him, since he was always tight with money, a characteristic reinforced by wartime conditions. (The much less well-off Anthony Powell had been astounded when, after he had stayed a few days at Rutland Gate, Henry accepted a check, which he had left—"far too much," his host protested in a note of thanks, "but very good of you in these hard times.")[75] The sums that Henry's writing brought him were never large, but he negotiated hard over them and meticulously acknowledged receipt of every check. Early in the war, a story earned three guineas from *New Writing* (the equivalent of a week's wages from his work as a fireman), ten guineas from the BBC.[76] Victory in a battle for an extra three shillings and sixpence for a BBC broadcast was announced triumphantly to John Lehmann,[77] who replied with gentle sarcasm, "My dear Henry, I am delighted to hear about the extra 3/6; it's the little things that count in the battle for prestige. News of it seems to have trickled out to the other authors who are getting rather disgruntled."[78] So it is striking how meekly Henry now paid £150 on account to Jacobson, Ridley & Co. of 68 Pall Mall,[79] which was pursuing a "Rose *v.* Rose clause" in the divorce case between Mary and Bunny Keene, which would bind the couple to silence, "burying their lurid and unhappy matrimonial history," as one of the senior lawyers involved wrote, "beyond resurrection by either of them."[80]

The proceedings dragged on over a couple of years. Even by the time they began, Henry and Mary's idyll had ended. Bereft, Henry fell into a deep depression, though the first signs about *Loving* were good. Five days before its publication date, the novel had sold its entire printing of five thousand copies—a clear indication that he had built up a readership of his own.[81] Among his fans was a contributor to *Penguin New Writing* named Jean MacGibbon, who had first written to him in 1942, with whom he corresponded over several years, and who gave him a good deal of encouragement—not least by reviewing him sympathetically. She became a joke among some of his friends: Rosamond Lehmann used *MacGibbonize* to mean *praise rhapsodically*. But most writers can benefit from a little MacGibbonizing, and in his dejection Henry more than ever needed all the support he could find.

One of those who were less than enthusiastic about *Loving* was Evelyn Waugh.[82] When *Brideshead Revisited* appeared, Green was struck by the coincidence that they had both written novels about country houses, and at Christmas he sent Waugh an enthusiastic but not uncritical letter about *Brideshead,* to which it seems Waugh did not reply.[83] In March, Green wrote again, repeating his praise but firming up his reservations: his regret at the deathbed repentance of Waugh's old reprobate Lord

Marchmain and his feeling that the character of the family nanny was overwritten.[84] "How curious it is," he added, "that we should both now be writing on lines essentially odious to each other. Me with servants and children, you with the dilemmas of the Church." He enclosed a second copy of *Loving* (the first had lain uncollected behind the porter's desk at the St. James's Club). "It's for old time's sake," he wrote, "because, alas, you wont like it." He signed the note, "Love from Henry." A week later, Waugh answered from White's—a grander club than the St. James's—at greater length and with less evident affection.[85] In his diary, Waugh wrote that he found *Loving* "obscene," but his letter began by telling Henry that he thought it very much better than *Caught:* "I am delighted to see your characters returned to privacy—fog-bound as they were in 'Party Going,' a complete, beleaguered world." He "loved" some of the minor characters, especially Miss Swift ("how dared I write of nannies?"), and the atmosphere of mutual suspicion and interrogation in the house. However, he soon turned to what he "hated": a long catalog that soon focused on points of consistency, accuracy, and especially social correctness. Would a lady speak like Mrs. Tennant? If her late husband had been a gentleman, wouldn't he have inherited Kinalty rather than bought it? "But it is a splendid book when I have said all I can say against it," he half concluded, before remembering something else: "You are debasing the language vilely."

To most readers of *Loving*, the language is among its main pleasures. It's partly a matter of what deceives as artlessness but also the way in which the anecdotal style is splashed with bravura passages, like one of Matthew Smith's paintings. Then, too, there is what V. S. Pritchett called the humility of Green's ear for his characters' speech[86]—humility, but humor also, as when Edith describes finding Violet sitting up naked in the bed in which Captain Davenport is hiding, "her fronts bobblin' at [me] like a pair of geese." As always with Green, it is a vulnerable kind of art, one that calls on the reader's understanding in more than the obvious ways and that has no ready answer to pedantry or plain instinctive dislike. Waugh's reaction shows something of what it had to contend with.

In his next book, Green was to go still deeper and risk still more, though with mixed success. He had begun it while *Loving* was in press, after Mary had taken Alice to Wales. "It's all about a man whose nerves are very bad," Henry told Rosamond Lehmann. He was already halfway through it, "having been blessed or cursed by a frightful surge of power & ideas. . . . The truth is that the present times are an absolute gift to the novelist. I see *everything* crumbling & growing all round me."[87]

"How soon d'you suppose they'll chuck you out?"

Olga, as she asked her husband this question, wore the look of a wounded animal, her lips were curled back from her teeth in a grimace and the tone of voice she used betrayed all those years a woman can give by proxy to the sawdust, the mirrors and the stale smell of public bars.

There's a resemblance to Cyril Connolly's prewar satires on the modern novel,[9] but the focus on drink is Green's own. In another radio talk on the novel, he describes the miniature dramas of "the pub I use at lunchtime near my office" (by contrast with "the other house I patronise at night").[10] It's as if drink and fiction—drink and experience itself—had for the moment come to seem synonymous to him. It was in 1948 that he first appeared in *Who's Who,* describing his recreation as "romancing over the bottle, to a good band." A year or two later, he told readers of the New York *Herald Tribune,* "I relax with drink and conversation."[11] But if an unfinished story written around this time, "The Great I Eye," is as autobiographical as it seems, the process, or at least its outcome, was not always so calm. Jim wakes with a hangover, still in evening dress:

His wife entered with a cup of tea. She placed it smack on a bed-side table next the telephone. She seemed to take care not to look at him.

He called her darling. In reply she said he had been too drunk last night, and waited, eyes averted. He said he knew.[12]

What follows is a panic-stricken fantasy in which he receives, or believes he receives, two compromising telephone calls about his previous night's activities, warning him that "he must tell his wife he was truly sorry." The postman arrives, bringing what Jim fears will be a pair of pink rubber false breasts but what are in fact—so far as there are any facts—a pair of initialed gold cuff links, which he hides from his wife "at the back of some used ties writhed into a knot like adders in the dark midden of discarded clothes." The chaos of ties acts as a metaphor for Jim's state of mind, in which what he remembers, or fears he remembers, from the previous night is a middle-aged, middle-class orgy. But was there really "a naked woman . . . humped on a sofa, the nudity in wait"? He—and we—can't be sure, partly because he can't remember but partly because the scene is so inextricable from his nightmare. At one point, the nude on the sofa "with a camel hump of thighs" becomes Jim's wife herself.

The title of "The Great I Eye" links the criminals' and servicemen's phrase "Eye! Eye!" warning that a policeman or some other authority figure is nearby, with an intenser paranoia suggested by the scrutiny of Jim's "halcyon eyeballs," which, themselves watched by a stuffed owl, gaze remorselessly down at their all-too-visible owner: "He thought there was never an excuse, for drink or anything. And one's body did not forgive. Always the same. The feeling it couldn't go on like it; misery, anxiety, death, death death."[13] In revealing so much of its author, the story also conveys something of what Dig had to deal with.

Not much was clear to Henry Yorke in these years, least of all what was going to become of Henry Green. At the most practical level, the official choices made over paper allocations did not imply a high valuation of literature. Green contributed a somewhat wild piece on the subject to a 1947 pamphlet entitled *The Battle of the Books,* which included articles by publishers, printers, and booksellers, as well as authors. He began with a show of businesslikeness: "The convertible value of a book . . . is high. A ton of books sells for more than a ton of bicycles, and fewer men are required in the process of manufacture." But the article soon degenerates into a barely coherent lament that art isn't appreciated and that paper rationing is a form of censorship: "The throttled moans of writers . . . are submerged in the dying stridency of the toilet paper people, the cigarette men, the paper handkerchief purveyors."[14] If the complaint about the incommensurability of literature and business is familiar enough, its personal implications for Green were unique. Paper restrictions postponed the Hogarth Press's long-mooted complete reissue of his novels. Meanwhile, his work for Pontifex seemed intolerable—even when he managed to get away from the office and from his father. In 1948, he went with a trade delegation on a two-month tour of Canada and "nearly went insane for lack of news from home."[15] What saved him, encouraging him to write his two final, extraordinarily controlled novels, was a breakthrough in the United States.

Concluding had appeared at the end of November 1948 and was taken by several literary editors as the opportunity for a retrospective as-

sessment of Green's work. "Regularly every two years or so a remarkable comet startles the darkness of the literary heavens," wrote Robert
Kee—already a prizewinning journalist—in the *Spectator.* "Accustomed
to the orthodox constellations, to a fixed recognisable North Star, but
above all to the darkness, earthbound traffic falters; people stop and
stare. It is another novel by Mr. Henry Green."[16] (Kee added a sly dig:
"Occasionally Mr. Green seems a little drunk with his own heady wine
and, like any drunk man, repeats himself and elaborates unnecessarily.")
The reviews were by no means uncritical, but American publishers, who
had more paper to spare than British ones, did not fail to notice that
everyone, including younger critics like Kee, treated Green as a major
artist, one of the leading experimentalists in English prose. In the *Lis-
tener,* George Painter observed in military style that Green had bravely
occupied "a forward area."[17] This was in a group review—one in which,
as it happened, *Concluding* took precedence over Evelyn Waugh's *The
Loved One*—but several other journals treated the book on its own,
among them the *New Statesman,*[18] *Time and Tide,*[19] and the *Spectator.*
Meanwhile, the Christmas issue of *The Times Literary Supplement* included a center-page essay on all of Green's work, focusing on his techni-
cal originality.[20]

One review that attracted attention in the States, and certainly the
one that pleased Green most, was by his friend Jean MacGibbon, writing
in *Horizon* as Jean Howard.[21] It is a long, exceptionally inward piece
about what Howard calls Green's "surprised exploration of the human
heart" and about the demands it makes on readers, both as a form of poetry and in its "close-range view of life." Her own response is not always
proportionate to what she is describing: It doesn't help to see *Concluding*
as an epic poem or its central character as embodying all of scientific hu-
manism. But Howard put forward a number of valuable interpretive insights and wrote interestingly about the book's element of panic, in the
classical sense as well as the modern one. *Concluding,* she argued, not
only tells the story of "the sadness and dignity of an old man" but also
contrives "to draw up from the deeper levels of the Unconscious . . . the
shadow of an allegory behind the individual, and places mankind in rela-
tion to the vast ill-comprehended landscape of his own time." Green told
her that this was "the only time I've seen anything printed about my
work which remotely attempts to describe what I'm trying to do." It had

made him cry "like a baby" that he should have had to wait twenty-two years for such recognition.[22] Less morosely, he wrote to Rosamond Lehmann, "The whole book seems to be having a real success, which is something to be savoured when one remembers the long hard road, so notably relieved by John & yourself ten years ago."[23] *Concluding* would not, after all, he reassured her, be his last book.

By February 1949, an agreement had been reached that Viking would publish *Loving* in the United States, followed by another of the novels, which at this stage looked likely to be *Concluding*. Viking also took an option on Green's next two books.[24] Although his first novels had appeared in the States two decades earlier, they had made little impression there at the time, and he was treated now as a discovery. The leading literary and intellectual journal in New York, *Partisan Review,* commissioned a four-thousand-word essay from Philip Toynbee that placed Green's novels in the tradition of high modernism. Toynbee wanted "to prepare American readers of Henry Green for the shock which they are almost bound to feel at their first approach to him. He is the most *self-conscious* of modern English novelists, the most mannered, the least digestible. I believe that he is also . . . among the most natural of our novelists and arguably the most important of them."[25] But as Ann Hancock has pointed out, the literary climate in which *Loving* appeared in New York was different from the one in Britain four years earlier. By now, readers had encountered Orwell's *Animal Farm* and *Nineteen Eighty-four,* Bellow's *The Victim,* Mailer's *The Naked and the Dead,* Camus' *The Stranger,* and Sartre's trilogy *Les Chemins de la liberté:* By comparison, *Loving* seemed gay, even escapist. *Harper's* asked for an extract and was made all the more eager when Green responded that it would suffer from being treated in this way and offered "The Lull" instead.[26] *Time,* tantalized by the idea of a pseudonymous writer of aristocratic origins who hated publicity, commissioned a profile.[27] Green colluded by accepting Viking's request that he come to New York for the launch of *Loving* in October, though he registered at the Gotham Hotel under a new and, given his sense of aging, ironic pseudonym: Mr. Yonge. Approached at a cocktail party by an editor who said, "Why, Henry Green! I never thought to see *you* here!" he replied, "You haven't. You have seen a ghost."[28]

His entrée to literary Manhattan was confirmed when one of the leading young American critics, Irving Howe, described *Loving* (again, in *Partisan Review*) as "completely successful . . . very funny and yet moving."[29] Green was interviewed for *The New York Times,* confiding that the main thing in life was "to get yourself right—not your health, but your brain" and that he used fiction as "a kind of solitary self-control." He also told the paper that the American novelist whom he most admired was Faulkner, and apparently a meeting was arranged.[30] Meanwhile, the *Time* profile suggested that "Hollywood could make of *Loving* a movie almost as stunning as the novel simply by faithfully following Green's sharp, quick series of glittering scenic plays and his natural, jumping dialogue."[31] Glittering *and* jumping: No wonder Harold K. Guinzburg, the Viking editor who had pushed the deal through, was able to tell Green that sales exceeded all expectation and that he hoped to see them top ten thousand copies by the end of the year.[32] In exaggerated anticipation of riches, Henry set up a tax-avoiding royalty trust for Dig and Sebastian.[33]

To John Lehmann, who had given Green so much support but whose new firm derived no profit from his success, it was all slightly galling. "They have done it again," he complained to his diary; "as in Christopher [Isherwood]'s case, I can remember struggling for years, during the war, to try & persuade the Americans they should publish Henry's books—but no, impossible, never would be understood. And now?—A literary triumph."[34] Still, some of the glow reflected on Lehmann, especially at literary parties at his home in South Kensington, where American writers were surprised to find that despite Green's reputed elusiveness, he could not only speak but make jokes. Some of his humor, as he liked to say, went "too far." At a dinner given by Lehmann in honor of Paul Bowles, Green talked without end, "keeping us all laughing" with his predictions about the invasion of Britain by blacks from the colonies, a prospect that he found intrinsically comical but one by which Dig was not amused.[35]

Meanwhile, Green was working on his next book. As usual, the process involved lamentation. In March 1949, he described himself to Mary Keene as "frightfully overworked & overstrained as I always get when doing [novels]."[36] On this occasion, some of the strain came from the sheer mechanics of construction in *Nothing,* the most traditional and technically the most accomplished of his works, and one that combines a

brilliant comic surface with a poignant analysis of aging, change, and uncertainty.

The novel is set in 1948, in a world very like Henry Yorke's. John
Pomfret, a widower of forty-five, is having an affair with the twenty-
nine-year-old Liz Jennings, a mixture, as it might be, of Jennifer Fry and
Mary Keene. We first encounter them in the dining room of a hotel over-
looking Hyde Park, which is also a favorite haunt of Jane Weatherby and
her suitor, Dick Abbot (whose quarrelsomeness, especially with waiters,
links him to Henry's friend Sylvester Gates, husband of his former mistress, Pauline).[37] Jane is a widow who had an affair with John Pomfret
while his wife was still alive and is still in love with him. She has a
twenty-year-old son, Philip, as well as a much younger daughter.[38]
Philip, it soon transpires, is seeing a lot of Pomfret's eighteen-year-old
daughter, Mary, who works in the same government-run information office.

One of the book's themes is the accommodations and adjustments
both of middle age in general and of formerly well-off people who have
lived through the war. John is always complaining about how hard
everyone, including Liz and Mary, has to work. After seeking financial
advice from the family lawyer, Jane has had "to take one of my little pills
and lie down." She has been forced, she says, to sell some of her jewelry.[39] Each laments to the other about the pinched, prosaic lives their
children lead and about the imaginative narrowing brought by economic
restrictions on foreign travel. These hardships are discussed, though, not
at work, where, in contrast with *Living, Caught,* and *Back,* the narrative
never ventures, but in more opulent surroundings, whether the hotel or
the older characters' homes in Knightsbridge: Jane's flat, where the Italian maid at last succeeds in producing John's favorite jugged hare; or
John's own place, where he gives Jane "what he called a scratch meal,"
"a spectacular supper . . . which began with caviar."[40] The shy, hardworking children, meanwhile, sit disapprovingly in park and pub:
"They're wicked darling," the priggish Philip Weatherby tells Mary
Pomfret. "They've had two frightful wars they've done nothing about
except fight in and they're rotten to the core."[41]

Green himself called this barbed social satire a comedy of manners,
and ever since it appeared there have been arguments over whether it is
more than that. Writing in the *Spectator* in May 1950, Marghanita Laski

called it "the very quintessence of triviality." She meant this as a compliment,[42] but in the *New Statesman,* John Richardson concluded that *Nothing* was a book "of no weight or importance."[43] Twenty-five years later, the novelist Paul Bailey described both it and Green's last novel, *Doting,* as "brilliant, but . . . rather arid and uninviting."[44] More recently still, Rod Mengham has argued that, in his last books, Green does little more than turn in on his own imaginary world, recapitulating earlier motifs as a prelude to lapsing into fictional silence.[45] To Green's older contemporary, L. P. Hartley, however—himself a novelist alert to the undertows of mannerly society—the novel meant more. Commenting on *Nothing*'s mixture of almost Edwardian traditionalism with up-to-date absurdism—"the contemporary fashion for making merry with material which in essence is sad and even tragic"—he pointed to a strong ambiguity in the title: "Is 'nothing' a trifle, a bagatelle, or is it the void, *le néant?* . . . I for one found it all too easy to slip through the glittering surface of the comedy into icy and terrifying depths."[46] His reaction was shared by some critics in the States, where, soon after the success of *Loving, Nothing* was published by Viking simultaneously with its appearance in Britain. Writing in *The New York Times Book Review,* Diana Trilling did not go as far as another American reviewer, who saw it as an allegory of British decline in international politics,[47] but she found "beneath the pleasant surface . . . a strikingly bold intelligence . . . and an acute knowledge of this wayward world": a world in which, she rightly says, there is little to choose between the selfishness of one generation and the priggishness of the next.

The book does not moralize in the direct way this analysis seems to imply. At the party that Jane gives for her son's twenty-first birthday, there are none of the authorial organ notes that are heard, for example, in T. S. Eliot's contemporary play, *The Cocktail Party.* One of Green's reasons for writing *Nothing* almost entirely in dialogue, he was to say, was precisely that people are misleading about themselves: It is by listening attentively to their lies and evasions, rather than to direct statements from outside, that we get to know them best. One of the older characters, asked by Mary whether her father and Jane had an affair, responds by saying, "Well I don't know about that. . . . We had our ups and downs. One can't be sure of anything. But what would be wrong if they had?"[48] Here as elsewhere, the approach is oblique because, as Green wrote soon after *Nothing* was published, "in life the intimations of reality are nearly always oblique."[49]

As in all his work, these intimations are keenly heard. "Really John," Liz Jennings says to Pomfret, ostensibly to stop him from interrogating his newly engaged daughter about her wedding, "when you're in love you can't make plans about one's plans."[50] This was the kind of sentence that brought criticism from linguistic conservatives such as Evelyn Waugh and Marghanita Laski.[51] Green's refusal of "correctness," in this respect, was an aesthetic choice as well as a matter of verisimilitude. "Good English," he said in an article published in 1950, is "a style preserved in the school-room and which has not changed in a hundred years, although the language currently spoken every day alters quicker than women's fashions. . . . In 'good English' the brain is dulled by clichés."[52] It was necessary for writers to escape not only linguistic patterns that had become worn out by others but those they would wear out for themselves if they did not continually experiment. He praised Joyce in this respect, and it is possible to hear an echo of Molly Bloom in Jane Weatherby—for example, in the hilarious vertigo of exaggeration, ignorance, fear, and complacency with which, before she is appeased by the idea of a trip to Brighton, she affects concern for her six-year-old daughter: "But the responsibility dear heart. You know what one comes across with those awful books of Freud's I haven't read thank God."[53]

Part of Green's art of revelation in *Nothing* lies in the many moments when different versions of a situation—different people's versions or different versions by the same person—are made to hint at quite other aspects of the story. John tells Liz that his old friend William Smith was deserted by his wife because he had lost both arms in a car crash. Liz's rival Jane, by contrast, who perhaps wants to draw attention to Liz's drinking habits, tells him it was mainly because Smith was a "soak": His wife "couldn't face pouring the whisky down his throat when he lost his arms."[54] John concedes that Smith drank, but in conversation with his recently engaged daughter warningly puts the blame on Mrs. Smith: "Drove poor William hopelessly to drink then left him when the poor fellow was done for."[55]

The joke here is not just the inconsistencies—elaborate steps in this dance of the sexes and generations—but the heartless comedy by which we have no access to the truth other than its interpretation by speakers who weren't involved and don't much care. Smith is dead; his wife is an offstage character, relevant only insofar as she is of use to Jane's scheming. Interpretive clues and nuances such as these have led to Green being compared to a detective writer, and the difficulty of understanding them correctly isn't confined to the novel's readers. It affects Jane herself, for example, when she wants to keep her younger child from knowing that the elder means to marry. What if the Italian maid should let the secret out? The child Penelope "absolutely jabbers in Italian now, so wonderful, while I can still hardly put two words together. And you see I don't understand what they say all the time. I spent hours with the dictionary to warn the woman not to breathe a word . . . and in the end perhaps I said the opposite, as one does."[56]

In saying the opposite, "as one does," Green's characters often inadvertently let out the truth. Talking to John about his affair with Liz, Jane warns him, "Oh my dear . . . you must be careful. Don't let it end as our love did in great country walks."[57] But of course she means "Do let it end" and that her own love for him isn't over. Sadnesses like this often break through in *Nothing*. Even horror is there, reinforcing everyone's sense of encroaching age—Jane's especially, but also Liz's fear of being left on the shelf, as well as John's diagnosis, one Henry Yorke had recently shared, of possible diabetes.[58] At the birthday party, an old name card for the dead William Smith finds its way into the *placement,* as if he were Banquo and *Much Ado About Nothing* had temporarily switched to *Macbeth.* However censorious Philip Weatherby may be of the way his elders live, his callow response at this moment shows little advance in sympathy. Jane tears up the card: " 'How odd and sad. . . . How dreadful' she murmured. 'Philip you didn't do this to me?' 'Never heard of the man' he replied."[59]

Nothing gives full rein to Henry Green's relish of black comedy, the "sick humor" that was soon to become fashionable. In another offstage joke-tragedy in the book, an old friend of everyone's dies, unexpectedly and almost disregarded, of a poisoned toe. Evelyn Waugh grumbled with some justice that the idea seemed to have been lifted from his *Decline and Fall,* where the schoolboy Tangent is accidentally grazed in the heel by a pistol bullet and, despite his mother's confident "that won't hurt him," perishes. But there is an important difference. In *Nothing,* the doomed Arthur Morris is a key to the past. He dies just as Mary Pomfret arrives at the nursing home to ask him about her dead mother. Mary has visited him before, with questions about her father's affair with Jane Weatherby. She wants to clear up the question that has also preoccupied Philip Weatherby since the beginning of their relationship. Could he be Mary's father's son? Are they in danger of marrying their half siblings? In those pre–DNA testing days, the mystery could not be solved. Reassurances are attempted by Arthur, by the narrative itself ("There was no resemblance physical or otherwise between Mr Weatherby and Mary"),[60] and by John, but all that his blusterings make clear is that no one knows—not even, perhaps, the author: At one point in both the manuscript and the final typescript, Philip Weatherby is called Philip Pomfret, a slip corrected only after it had been queried by the copy editor.[61]

All this echoes one of the preoccupations of *Caught* and *Back*. Unconscious incest is—as in the *Oedipus* trilogy—the most powerful of metaphors for human unknowing and the most symmetrical of plotting devices. Both aspects are dominant in *Nothing*. And if the novel's past is elusive, so also are its present and future. There is a traditional element of narrative tension in this: How will the older couples shake out? And will Philip's engagement to Mary hold? But the book also, as we have seen, touches on contemporary concerns about the limitations of even fictional knowledge, never more plaintively than at the end of the party at which the engagement is announced, when Philip and Mary "danced again and again until, as the long night went on they had got into a state of unthinking happiness perhaps."[62]

Green intended this as one of the novel's climaxes. As if to heighten, or compensate for, its view of the untidiness of human information, *Nothing* is constructed with a Noël Coward–like formality quite new in Green's work. With rare exceptions, each of the brief episodes is based on a conversation between two people. Green had experimented with such duets earlier—for example, in the middle section of *Caught*. Now he pushed them to the limit. Almost every possible pairing of the characters is explored in three carefully modulated movements. Each main section ends with a scene between John Pomfret and Jane Weatherby and is separated from the next by a blank page, as required by a note in the manuscript.[63] The first and third movements open with Pomfret and Liz Jennings; the middle one, very dramatically, with the novel's only sustained passage of description: the hotel room before the party, empty of people—mirrors and chandeliers reflecting each other into infinity. It is this movement that includes the words about the couple's "happiness perhaps." Green's manuscript asked for a minor interval here: "Leave a whole half page blank please" (an instruction missed by his typist,[64] so that the copyeditor's note to the typesetter stipulated only the usual scene division, five lines of white space). In a pattern so artificial, it is noticeable that this sentence—the apex of Mary and Philip's relationship, and the point at which so many of the novel's doubts are simply gathered—comes exactly halfway through the novel.[65]

Green, of course, had always relished such precarious points of balance. *Nothing* is full of them, from the end of the first scene, when Liz leaves the hotel, "her sad face beaming,"[66] to the tragicomic tender selfishness of the ending:[67]

> "Well Jane" [John] said with a sort of low-pitched assurance, then yawned a fifth time, "our children will just have to work their own lives out, we can't do everything for them."
>
> She gave no answer. . . .
>
> There was a longer pause while his eyelids drooped.
>
> "And how's your wicked diabetes my own darling?" she whispered.
>
> "All right" he barely answered.
>
> "And is there anything at all you want my own?"
>
> "Nothing . . . nothing" he replied in so low a voice she could barely have heard and then seemed to fall deep asleep at last.

The passage parodies Henry's own drowsy kind of dependency. Because his egotism was more needy than imperious, it drew people to him, but there was a degree of ruthlessness in it, which Mary Keene had discovered and was to encounter again. They had stayed on good terms, but not so good as to lead him to help her financially when she became pregnant by Matthew Smith in 1949. Smith did not want the child, and the couple separated—temporarily, as it was to turn out—but meanwhile Mary was alone and asked Henry for help with hospital fees for the delivery.[68] He told her that the little money he had left after taxation was taken up by the education of Sebastian, who was now at Eton. Besides, the new baby (who, in the event, died of a heart defect within days of being born) was not his responsibility. Meanwhile, he agreed to help her with something she was trying to write for a film. Her reply was sympathetic, if not entirely unironic about his "being broke": "It seems horribly sad that we are all in trouble now."[69]

HE WAS TO FORM A HAPPIER RELATIONSHIP THE FOLlowing year, one that was founded on two quite brief encounters but that lasted imaginatively for the rest of his life. In April 1950, Eudora Welty was in London to promote a collection of stories, *The Golden Apples*— the fifth of her books to be published in Britain. She did the literary rounds and met with her share of the superciliousness that Englishmen tended to adopt toward all Americans and woman writers and especially those who had the misfortune to be both. In the English way, no one told her anything about the people she met. At one party, she was introduced to Anthony Powell—then a publisher as well as a novelist, but not yet famous—who she gathered from the conversation had written a book. She asked him its title. He answered loftily, "That question is not asked."[70] Later, another man who came in—also evidently an author—was applauded by everyone. Undeterred by her previous rebuff, she asked the unaskable question and was only half surprised in this Lewis Carroll world to be told that he had written nothing.

It took her some time to realize that *Nothing* was in fact a title and that the dark-haired, rather deaf, shyly uproarious novelist was the author, too, of *Loving*, then at the height of its American succès d'estime. She had read it on the boat coming over and was still under its spell. When she realized she was talking to Henry Green, she was "bowled over." The reaction was mutual. In conventional terms, the forty-one-year-old Welty was no beauty, but she was slender, vivacious, and responsive—a great laugher. John Lehmann wrote in his diary, "Henry & Eudora flung themselves at one another, & I have never seen Henry work so hard, be so recklessly, madly ebullient. . . . E. drank more & more & was completely swept off her feet."[71]

The next day, in his offhand-seeming, self-preoccupied fashion, Green rang Welty at her hotel in Bloomsbury: "I'm staying in tonight—

why not come over? I have a toothache." As she arrived at Trevor Place, she met Dig on her way out to a party. Eudora was shown into Henry's study, where they sat in front of a fire and talked about "heaven knows—everything, I think. I cannot remember. I was captivated." She found Henry "just fine. He was a terribly attractive man, of course." He had "such a sweetness," a mixture of spontaneity, mischief, and humor, "a hilarious streak that goes all through his work. And he had that wonderful sudden laugh, just explosive."

They turned out to have a surprising amount in common. Both were the children of successful businessmen. Welty herself had attended the Columbia University business school, but when her father died suddenly in 1931 she had left in order to earn her living through journalism, including radio journalism. Her assignments took her the length and breadth of Mississippi during the Depression—experiences similar in their impact on her work to those of Henry Green in the factory and the Fire Service. Like Green's, Welty's work often mixes a lyrical narrative style with an interest in the lives and talk of "ordinary" people. She revered and had learned from Faulkner, as well as Virginia Woolf, and had admiringly reviewed the work of Henry's Fire Service friend William Sansom.[72] Like Green, she believed in the necessary separateness of any writer: "The author, who writes at his own emergency, remains and needs to remain at his private remove. I wished to be, not effaced, but invisible."[73] Meanwhile, her occasional introduction of mythical elements such as the Pan-like figure of King Maclain in *The Golden Apples,* with his seduction of the town's maidens, has resemblances in *Concluding* and reflects a bohemian side to Welty's superficially conventional personality: At Columbia, she had hung out in nearby Harlem. She was to write later, "A sheltered life can be a daring life as well. For all serious daring starts from within."[74] This attitude made another link between her and Green, who—toothache forgotten—took her on a pub crawl, in the course of which he introduced her to Pimm's, perhaps thinking it the English equivalent of mint julep. He talked about his recent trip to the States (she mainly recalls him telling her that American air-conditioning systems were "altogether wrong" from the perspective of a manufacturer of distilling apparatus, because they were wasteful of water, which they should have recycled). She talked about his work, and he told her he thought

Pack My Bag was the best thing he had written but that she would never be able to find a copy.

Welty remembered the whole evening as "just like a direct hit." When she got home, she read everything Green had published. They never met again, yet the feeling between them remained intense. Ten years later, she wrote an essay about his work, prompting a flurry of correspondence that, on his side at least, reads like a series of love letters.[75] Welty and Elizabeth Bowen, whom she also met on the same trip, were always to refer to him in their conversations as "the loving Henry Green."

Not everyone was so beguiled. Evelyn Waugh, in particular, was by now waging a campaign against Henry among their acquaintances. When Nancy Mitford mentioned to Waugh how much she was enjoying *Nothing,* he replied that he "thought nothing" of it and tore into what he described as its unidiomatic dialogue:

> What Henry never did for a moment was to define his characters' social position. Sometimes they spoke "Mrs Chichesterese" [a reference to the genteel Pamela Chichester], sometimes Air Force, sometimes sheer Gloucester peasant—"Leave me be": "Whyever for." He has just lost his ear through spending so much time with low-class women. . . . "I'll take a sherry." "Phone me" all the joke-charade vulgarities. Well Etonians of 45 don't talk like that. . . . I daresay Henry never could write dialogue at all & has been bluffing all the time. I mean, we have all said "how wonderfully Henry has caught real proletarian speech" while all the time it was just as false as his "Knightsbridge" characters. . . . Well it's a rotten book.[76]

Waugh may have been a little envious of the novel's success in the States, though he denied this. (He may also have been nervous about his own recently completed *Helena,* a weak book that was nevertheless a hit in America later that year.) As far as language was concerned, Waugh was well off target: There was far more variety than he cared to think in how people of all classes talked in the newly demotic England of the 1950s. The social world to which he attended, of course, was confined principally to the English aristocracy, expatriates, and European nobility like those with whom he had recently been hobnobbing in Paris chez Mitford and in Rome.[77] His attacks on Green were part of his long campaign against modernity—and also, perhaps, a sign of the mental instability that was to become more pronounced in the coming years.[78] The onslaught continued with mounting comic extravagance. The following spring, the Yorkes spent "a very long week-end" with the Waughs at Piers Court, where at their first meal Henry incensed his host by asking if he might smoke before everyone had finished eating. Though it was a common enough practice at the time, Waugh pushed his plate forward "to the full extent of his arms in order to register his protest over this breach of decorum."[79] When, in a letter to Waugh written soon afterward, Nancy Mitford mentioned Ingrid Wyndham, the daughter of a cousin of Henry's, Waugh replied that being a member of that family was "not a thing to go into light-heartedly":

> In London, where everyone is seedy, [Henry] did not appear notable. Here in the country he looked GHASTLY. Very long black dirty hair, one brown tooth, pallid puffy face, trembling hands, stone deaf, smoking continuously throughout meals, picking up books in the middle of conversation & falling into maniac giggles, drinking a lot of raw spirits, hating the country & everything good. If you mention Forthampton to him he shies with embarrassment as business people used to do if their businesses were mentioned.
>
> Poor Dig very cowardly, quite belying her great moustaches, gentle, lost. She has picked up a whole proletarian argot which she employs with an exquisitely ladylike manner. I really think Henry will be locked up soon. Dig's brother is locked up already. It is a poor lookout for their wretched son.[80]

The Yorkes subsequently visited Mitford in Paris, where, she reported, her old friend Henry behaved charmingly and surprised her by speaking excellent French.[81] Nothing daunted, Waugh returned to the attack later the same year, telling Mitford that the habits of the pub-haunting characters in Graham Greene's *The End of the Affair* "are *precisely* and in *every detail identical* with those of the Bright Young Yorkes."[82] And to Maurice Bowra he comically fantasized that Henry was a closet communist:

> Evidence: love of false names and clandestine travel; membership of Fire Brigade; insistence in all his works that social distinctions depend solely on cash; close trade relations, including introducing water-closets to the Kremlin; dependence on jazz bands; ostentatious poverty (mulcted for party funds); hatred of architecture, wine and poetry; elaborate code of conventional bad-manners in dress, opening doors to women, etc; obsession with royal family (most disrespectful).[83]

"Clandestine travel" may have been a reference to Green's trip to the States as "Mr. Yonge." He continued to be unpredictable in his responses to personal attention from readers. In 1950, an American graduate student was rebuffed when he wrote to the Hogarth Press asking various questions, such as whether Green was married and, if so, whether his wife was living. Green's publishers themselves often fared little better. When the Norwegian house Gyldendal, which brought out *Loving* and *Nothing* in 1951, asked for biographical information, its staff was told firmly that "Mr. Green does not care for personal publicity, and we have neither biographical notes nor photographs of him."[84] At the party to launch *Nothing* in London, Henry and Dig fell into conversation with Eve Perrick of the *Daily Express* without realizing that she was a gossip columnist. Afterward, Henry wrote frantically to his new editor at Hogarth, Norah Smallwood, "I suppose there is no way of stopping her now, but she alarmed me by talking to Dig about this firm being sanitary engineers—a thing we ceased to be ten years ago. Any tie-up between my novels and my career is, I think, harmful to me."[85] Yet whether because Smallwood persuaded him differently, because he minded less about how he was seen in America, or just because he himself was ambivalent about the matter, only a few months later he told another journalist, "Say, I am the son of a prominent industrialist. Say, I am an engineer in the firm."[86] And in 1952 he not only gave a full interview at Pontifex's London office to Nigel Dennis for *Life* magazine but allowed the magazine to use photographs.[87]

Some of the pictures were specially taken for the article: a moody, sidelong shot of him sitting at a bar in an overcoat, cigarette in hand, hiding his face, as well as a series pantomiming self-concealment: Henry with his long hands covering his eyes, or from behind as he scratches his head, stretches his back, and fools around with his hat. But the feature also included photographs of his wedding and of the Birmingham factory, which must have been provided by himself or by Dig, with whom he appears full face, reaching for a drink, in a pleasantly unposed shot in what seems to be a hotel lounge.

The most revealing touches in the interview, though, are not the pictures but moments in the conversation whose importance Nigel Dennis himself doesn't seem to have picked up. When he mentioned that his subject was "soberly dressed," Henry suggested that *sadly* would be a more appropriate adverb. It was one of several clues both about insobriety and about sadness. He spoke of living his life to "the small full" and of "the aching shallows" of the experience of middle age. Meanwhile, he said that he liked "to do my own drinking" and claimed that his daily intake of gin—modestly estimated at half a bottle—kept him in good health, though he admitted to his ulcer.

Once again, Green explained that he wrote "to get myself straight," a process that he compared with distillery: piping off "the things that are in ferment." He talked about his determination to create a new kind of fiction, and about jazz—especially the singer and pianist Mildred Bailey, the swing bandleader Chick Webb, and his regret at having missed a chance to hear Jelly Roll Morton in New Orleans in 1928. But he detested artistic conversation, he told Dennis: "It is absurd to waste good talk on topics, such as art, which come after life, not before it." It was a writer's duty "to meet as many pedestrian people as possible and to listen to the most pedestrian conversation." Then, as if to practice what he preached, he turned to "heat balances, second-and-third-effect evaporators, stripping columns and reflux condensers," his recent election as chairman of the British Chemical Plant Manufacturers' Association, his wish to see Sebastian succeed him in the business, and finally his views on taxation. If there was any link between Henry Yorke the industrialist and Henry Green the novelist, Dennis concluded, it would have been visible to the tax collector.

It was still ostensibly for tax reasons that Green continued to evade the question of his books' appearing in paperback. In May 1951, Evelyn Waugh mischievously suggested to Eunice Frost at Penguin that Green might like to be included on their list.[88] She wrote to him straightaway, saying how delighted she would be and reminding Green that Penguin had approached him several times before, "only to get the impression that you were disinclined to want a wider audience." Green replied, "Mr. Evelyn Waugh thinks wrong" and suggested that they return to the issue when and if there was a reduction in income tax.[89] The redoubtable Frost persisted: Could they make a postdated arrangement now?[90] Green said he could not consider the notion until "perhaps 5 or 10 years time."[91] Frost replied, with a hint of satire, "I shall put it on record, then, to approach you in five or ten years' time."[92] But in the general election of October 1951, Labour was defeated by a Conservative Party committed to lowering taxes.[93] The following year, Green signed an agreement with Penguin for *Loving*.[94]

─────────

CHAPTER 10

Last Love

ONE EVENING IN SEPTEMBER 1951, DIG FOUND HER-
self counting some silver spoons that had been given to her and Henry as
a wedding present twenty-two years earlier. It wasn't an anniversary of
any kind, but she was approaching fifty, and there were other reasons for
her to take stock of her life, in however oblique a fashion. She had just
learned that King George VI, whose wife was an old friend of hers, was
suffering from cancer and likely to die soon, in his mid-fifties. Sebastian
was about to leave school and start his military service: What would the
future hold for him? Henry, meanwhile, had been busy completing a new
novel and was deep in the latest of his romances, again with a much
younger woman: Kitty Freud, whose brief marriage to the painter Lucian
was falling apart. When Dig found that six of their spoons were missing,
she was suddenly inconsolable.[1] It may have been the only time that she
allowed her feelings to overwhelm her, and it seems perfectly possible
that even she did not understand why. As for Henry Yorke, to judge from
his account of the incident in a letter to Kitty, it seems that—whether out
of infatuation or merely with the occasional obtuseness that marked him
off from Henry Green—he found it baffling.

Henry had met Kitty at a party at Cyril Connolly's house in Regent's
Park.[2] She was in her mid-twenties, very thin, with vulnerable eyes and a
quick, shy smile, extremely intelligent and well read. She had loved his
work ever since she read *Blindness* as a teenager, when she identified

strongly with the character of Joan, daughter of the tempestuous defrocked parson. As a girl, Kitty—whose father was the sculptor Jacob Epstein, a close friend of Matthew Smith—hated school, read voraciously, and always wanted to draw and paint. During the war, she studied at the Central School of Art and, while still in her teens, was briefly involved with the poet and novelist Laurie Lee. Since one of her numerous pretty and flirtatious young aunts had had a long affair with him, this caused a certain amount of drama in the family, but Kitty was not deterred. The same aunt had been a lover of Lucian Freud, too, and it was through her that they met.

Lucian was twenty-six when they married, Kitty twenty-one. She soon gave birth to a daughter, Annie. The couple's first year together was very happy, and Lucian's portraits of her are unusually tender, at least by his own harsh standards. But he was not a man for home life or for nursing anyone else's sensitivities. When not attending to their household in Saint John's Wood, Kitty had to keep up with a Soho nightlife that she no longer enjoyed but in which she did not dare leave her husband to his own devices. "We just used to drink until we fell over," she said later with faint incredulity, "and terrible scenes broke out with people taking absolutely no notice." In the marginally soberer, more intellectual company of the Connollys and their friends she was no more at ease, finding them "snobbish and treacherous," so it was a relief to find that a novelist whose work she so much liked not only was not at all patronizing but understood and seemed to share her vulnerability.

She and her baby were soon frequent visitors to Trevor Place, where Dig made her welcome and Henry read aloud to her from the novel he was writing. The house struck her as tiny, though at a fashionable address, and she came to wonder whether there was any connection with stories she heard about Henry's being stingy. When he asked her out to dinner, mutual friends joked that he always recommended skate rather than lobster to his girlfriends. Perhaps because she never ate much, she did not notice. Henry wasn't ungenerous to her with presents, but what she principally wanted from him was what she got: his company, his affection, his jokes. They sometimes met at the George IV, where she would find him drinking with cronies such as Arthur Koestler, who had recently moved to Montpelier Square, A. J. ("Freddie") Ayer, Francis Wyndham, or Matthew Smith's new fan and middleman, Roald Dahl. If it was evening, the two of them would go on to dinner at a nightclub. They danced only once, Henry swaying politely "in that old-fashioned 1930s way." Mostly, they just talked. He was sympathetic about the difficulties between her and Lucian, and she was fascinated by the gap between the utter conformity of Henry and Dig's milieu, which she felt she was glimpsing just as it was about to vanish forever, and his private existence as a writer. Henry talked to her a lot not only about his books but about his work at Pontifex—Kitty listening, with a degree of attention that Dig had never found easy to muster, to laments about office quarrels and about orders not having come through. There was a distinct difference, she noticed, between Henry Yorke, who could be very grand and rather sharp, surprising people by putting them in their place, and the sympathetic, unthreatening Henry Green. What united the two personalities, and what she liked best, was that the depression she always sensed under the surface, and which served as one of the affinities between him and her, was never allowed to dominate, wasn't deployed as "revealing *angst*" but was masked by Henry's sense of comedy and his curiosity about everything outside himself.

They were both, she felt, pessimists, "living on the edge," but he found ways of showing her how situations that she thought tragic could be funny. Once, he took her miles out on the Underground to see the Russian State Circus. There was an act involving bears of different sizes on bicycles. The leading bear missed its footing and fell off, causing the others to fall into disarray. A trainer came in and tried to get the animals back onto their machines, but they couldn't keep going. Unlike Kitty, Henry thought it all hilarious. "It made the excursion for him." Another time, he sent her a newspaper picture of a performing dog standing on its hind legs, balancing on its head a pile of saucers, one of which was out of kilter so that the whole edifice was obviously about to topple. He added a note: "This is your predicament, darling—and mine."

Self-deprecation was an important element in his jokes. He had become conscious of being overweight, and another of his animal anecdotes concerned an elephant that had slipped out of a sling while being unloaded at the docks and had fallen twelve feet, mercifully without injury. Henry told Kitty he was on the track of a press photograph "of afterwards when she's lying on the ground getting her breath back—she weighs over one ton—with a man kneeling before her stroking her huge forehead."[3] Since Kitty was pregnant again, she might have taken the story amiss. As always, Henry was liable to go too far, one way or another. His letters often included apologies—needless, Kitty felt—for having been "tiresome" or "overtired."[4] But for the most part they were an affectionate mixture of gossip and comic fantasy. The news of George VI's illness left him dry-eyed. "The King is obviously going to die, God bless him," he wrote. "It follows that there will be the FUNERAL—(tears)— six months later the CORONATION—(joy). Then Q[ueen] Mary will die—(more tears)—and P[rincess] Margaret will get married—(tears). This is what the next three years will bring."[5] More exuberantly, he pretended to imagine Kitty in Wales, where she had gone to get away from Lucian, sitting naked for an outdoor portrait "in the first flurry of snow with a donkey nibbling at your hair" or, no less improbably, "eating the most huge meals—mountain lamb, asphodel honey and deep gold butter. Do you ever think of us down below?"[6]

By this time, they had been together for about a year and a half. Rationally speaking, there had never been any question in Kitty's mind of the relationship's becoming any more than an affair. As always with his girlfriends, Henry had delivered a preemptive warning that—in her words—"he was devoted to Dig and never wanted to be married to anybody else." Kitty was very familiar with the rules governing such arrangements. Her father had remained married throughout his still-continuing affair with her mother, Kathleen Garman, who had in all three children by him. Another containing element was Dig herself, who made Kitty feel that Trevor Place was a second home, so that "quite apart from him being a lover *they* were very important to me as a family, because I felt terribly outcast." At the same time, Dig showed in an unspoken way what her house rules were: in essence, no overexplicitness but no hypocrisy either. To Kitty, the setup seemed like something out of Henry James: Dig was "a very exceptional woman. She had a curious, accepting insouciance about her. She sort of sailed through and past everything. Nobody knew whether she knew, and it would have been outrageous to have ever indicated or hinted at it." Kitty was anyway too absorbed in her own unhappiness to speculate much about Dig's underlying feelings. But another brake on the affair, from Kitty's point of view, was the difference of age. So it was possible for her to believe that she hoped for no more with Henry than she already had, that "I simply wanted to be adored, and I was." But so close a relationship could not escape complication and ambivalence, and her deepest feelings were often closer to those that she remembered from Chekhov's story "Lady with Lapdog": "something that started lightly and without any idea of continuing turned into something lengthy, painful, difficult and insoluble."[7]

Henry was agonizingly possessive of her. A. J. Ayer overheard Henry at a party in Eaton Square denounce him to her "as a notorious seducer and pleading with her not to go out with me."[8] But her pregnancy brought home to both of them that the affair, at least in its present intensity, should end. Gradually, if not without relapses, it did. Poppet John, who was about to embark on what was to be a very successful marriage, seems to have had a hand in pointing out to Henry the realities of the situation: among them, perhaps, that, once the Freuds had divorced, Kitty would need to find a husband close to her own age, for her children's sake as well as her own. Henry had told Kitty, "Everything you do is for the worst"—first marrying Lucian, then getting pregnant just as they were splitting up. Now he tried to help her do something for the best and for herself. In November, John wrote to "Darling Darling Henry" that although "I don't really think it was *me* that stopped it," she was glad that some kind of a change had occurred without breaking his heart. She added that the "awful thing is that ones heart gets a bit tough as times go by."[9] But last love can be as powerful as first, and Henry's heart was never to toughen toward Kitty. Years later, he talked to people who hadn't known them at the time as if she was still among the most important elements in his life.

While Henry was preoccupied with Kitty and with *Doting,* Sebastian had been growing up fast. By 1952, "Debo" Devonshire was telling her sister Nancy Mitford that Sebastian was "a genius, an all round masterpiece of nature." (She was a little put out that spring when he declined an invitation to come and stay with the family in Ireland and they somehow found themselves entertaining his parents, instead.)[10] Henry was very fond of his son, but as with any adolescent child there had been difficulties on both sides. Sebastian later described school holidays—much of which he had spent with his grandparents or at the homes of friends—as having involved various tensions when he was at Trevor Place, particularly the "ghastly business of going to a play or a musical, or going out to a nightclub. I always used to have to ask some daughter of friends of my parents, and it was always a great thing about who was going to be asked, and I absolutely hated the whole thing, and I didn't really want to be there at all."[11] Sebastian's feelings about these excursions combined teenage shyness with the difficulty of being overshadowed by his charming father. The dynamics of such situations enter into Green's last novel.

The main couple in *Doting,* the Middletons, resemble Henry and Dig but without Henry Green's writing. Arthur is a businessman in his forties, stout, unhealthy, inclined to drink too much; Diana is a full-time wife. They have brought up their only child in the way the Yorkes and everyone they knew did, sending him to an expensive boarding school, where he has learned to revere sportsmen and to fear and despise poets.[12] On the first and last nights of the school holidays that give the novel its frame, the parents take the adolescent boy to a nightclub. The entertainment on the first occasion is a juggling act; on the second, it is to be wrestling, but the wrestlers fail to materialize. Between the event and the nonevent, Peter is sent off to Scotland to catch fish, his achievements at which give his doting parents some vicarious, conciliatory excitement.

The Middletons' doting on Peter is a main source of the book's title. "We are not to enter into a competition as to who dotes on him most!" Arthur exclaims to Diana. "Oh, doting!" she replies, in what is described as "tones of disgust." Her response hints at her attitude to another focus of Arthur's doting, the nineteen-year-old Annabel Paynton, but a question is asked throughout the book about the differences between doting and loving. Where *Loving* had explored with indulgence as well as amused skepticism the baffling exhilarations of romance, *Doting* adopts—and lightly satirizes—a more resigned, more middle-aged view, in which loving is seen less as an emotion than as a set of habits—habits such as the bath-and-bedtime routines of Arthur and Diana, with their prosaic intimacy:

> At last she heard him coming, undress in the bathroom and then, almost before she knew it . . . he was climbing cautiously in between the sheets.
>
> "Finished darling?" she murmured when he had settled.
>
> "All finished" he answered.
>
> There was a pause.

"Asleep?" she asked in a low voice, without turning over towards him.

"Not yet" he said.

"So wonderful" she immediately went on "really wonderful to have Peter back!"

What's implied by *doting*, in contrast, is a juvenile infatuation—or, as in Arthur's case with Annabel, a middle-aged relapse into one. The person who uses the expression most is Annabel herself. (" 'Come on' she said with a challenge. 'Let's talk of doting. Tell me how you first met Diana.' ") She seems to have picked it up from her poet friend Campbell Anthony. But when, in a prepostmodern moment, she tells Arthur that Campbell is preparing an anthology of love poetry that he intends to call *Doting*, the older man says disapprovingly—notwithstanding his use of the word in conversation with Diana later—"Well, you know doting, to me, is not loving. . . . Loving goes deeper."[13]

As so often with Green's work, it is difficult, out of context, to convey the intricacy of meaning in this apparently simple exchange. Arthur's feelings for Annabel and hers for him are complicated by his reactions to what she has been saying not only about her boyfriends but about her parents, who have recently separated and who never appear in the book but who influence what happens—not least because of their long relationship with the Middletons. Further, the daughterless Arthur has feared, ever since Annabel was a small girl, that his affection for her might arouse suspicion. In all this, the disparity between Arthur's and Annabel's ages adds another dimension to the meaning of *doting*. Green, who loved quaint usages, may have known that *doting* had once meant decaying like a tree; a dotard is a silly old fool because he is a tree that has lost its top branches. As the Middletons' friend Charles Addinsell says, "Nothing ever gets better . . . not at our age."[14]

This is the disillusioned perspective from which Peter's teenage behavior is judged. It is as if in *Doting* Green is writing at the opposite pole from the *Kunstlerroman* of *Blindness*. Peter is funnily well observed, especially his hoarse incredulity when Annabel reveals that his school hero Terry Shone ("only the best half back we've had in years") likes to write. Peter's resistance to poetry is one of the many differences between him and his aesthetic counterparts John Haye in *Blindness* and Dick Dupret in *Living*, versions of their author at the equivalent stages. And his main role in the novel is not, like them, to embark on a life of his own but to highlight a phase of his parents' marriage and their uncertainty about what will come next. While their son has been growing up, the Middletons have changed, though not so much as the world around them. There's no sense that the past is preferable to the present: When Annabel tries to elicit some anecdotes from Arthur about his first meeting with Diana, he eventually admits that it occurred at a hunt ball; yet his present ambience of Knightsbridge flats and restaurants doesn't make him nostalgic for the Edwardian country houses of his youth. And while the two seem to find no consolation in memory, they also show little interest in the future. When Diana asks, "D'you really think we are making the best of our lives?" all Arthur can answer is that he's doing what he can.

Green had always written with a kind of intent, part-baffled sympathy toward women, but *Doting* is unique in its attention to the life of a married woman of Dig's generation and class. In this scene, Diana admits "almost in a whisper" that she is bored. By the end of the book, her voice has become stronger. Peter wants to know when the promised wrestlers will appear. She replies:

> "In their own good time, I suppose. Like everyone else. . . . As you go on in life, I fear you'll find people come more and more only to consult their own convenience."
>
> "But if they're paid to appear?" Peter wanted to be reassured.
>
> "Aren't we all, in one way or another, darling, being paid, the whole of the time? Take tonight. Don't we all have an obligation to your father because he is taking us out in this expensive place?"

Like *Nothing*, *Doting* is constructed with symmetrical formality, and these reasonable discontents of Diana's are balanced by those of Annabel and her friend Claire, young single women with jobs who are no less puzzled and thwarted by their dealings with older men, while finding boys of their own age little more interesting than Peter.[15] (Annabel complains vividly that "these endless Campbells and Terences just don't exist yet. . . . All they do is to use you with their parents. One's an excuse to borrow the car.")

For Annabel, as for many of Green's characters, the problem is part of the larger one of human separateness and ignorance, the gaps between how others see themselves and how they behave: "What do we ever really learn about other people? . . . Not to trust the way they look, and that's about all." *Doting* doesn't have a single, simple meaning, and not all of the pessimistic views expressed in it are borne out. The adulteries that seem on the brink of taking place between Arthur and Annabel and between Diana and Charles never occur, however much Arthur's claim that "Di and I don't fib to one another" has been eroded. And since one of the book's balancing acts is between doting and loving, it is important that the only true love scenes take place between Arthur and Diana. The comic bathos of their early domestic episodes is balanced by the occasions when they go to bed to make love,[16] and when the word *love* is quietly insisted on, not only by Diana ("Oh heavens, how I love you, God help me") but—with extra force, given Green's abstemiousness in this respect—by the narrative itself, which speaks of her "tones of love" and how she "let her lovely body be undressed." Though Kitty Freud believed that Henry and Dig "had long ceased to have any sexual side to their marriage," it is hard not to read these passages as reflecting something closer to the truth about them—perhaps the most important truth.

Nothing much happens in *Doting*. Continuity, especially in the negative sense that most of the dramas in most people's lives fail to transform anything, had always been a main theme of Green's fiction, and in *Doting* this sense is reinforced by what V. S. Pritchett, reviewing the novel in *The New Yorker*, described as its subdued tone, which is related in turn to its interest in "the blurred, the lethargic, inarticulate part of human beings, the wound that becomes their quotidian poetry."[17] Green's characters are puzzled, slow-witted; they feel their predicaments strongly but have little power to express, let alone alter, them. Pritchett sees this as a result of "the injury done to certain English minds by the main, conventional emphases of English life." The Middletons' conversation is "beautifully inadequate to their condition," in which they find themselves making personal accommodations and "arrangements" as substitutes for more sustaining values.

Certainly, the book provides a droll, unusually closely observed critique of a class and of the ways in which it maintains and transmits its conventions. Perhaps Annabel, Claire, and Peter are all a little more knowing by the end. The widower Charles may to some extent have been jogged out of his pessimistic apathy. Diana has learned something about Arthur and has manipulated it adroitly so as to preserve the status quo. After the party at the nightclub, when the drunken Charles asks Arthur, "Will it be all right tomorrow?" Arthur replies simply, "Of course." In all this, what Henry Green has achieved resembles the juggling act described in the opening scene:

> the ball supporting a pint pot, then the pint pot a second ball until, unnoticed by our party, the man removed his chin and these separate objects fell, balls of ivory each to a hand, and the jug to a toe of his patent leather shoe where he let it hang and shine to a look of faint surprise, the artist.

The passage is surely a metaphor for Green's own work, and there may be more irony than at first appears in the fact that the climax is "unnoticed by our party," a phrase in which the pronoun itself is left hanging and shining in the air, poised ambiguously between "the party that you, the reader, and I, the narrator, have been observing together" and "the party that (in real life) I was a member of." Either way, the point is that at his supreme moment, the artist is ignored.

Henry Green himself had this feeling. Increasingly, the struggles involved in the process were becoming too much for him. In *Doting* even more than in his other books, it is easy to mistake the apparent naïveté of the composition for casualness. The book is erratic and can be clumsy, but its air of guilelessness was hard-won. The final text had taken a year and a quarter to complete, with Green doing his best to write a thousand words a day, sometimes at lunchtime, sometimes at night after the pub and dinner.[18] The working title had been "Adoring," but around the time of the shift in his relationship with Kitty, Henry altered the word to *doting* wherever it occurred in the manuscript.[19] Like this crucial change, most of the other corrections—made in blue ink in Green's small, clear hand—however slight-seeming, increase the book's sharpness. On the last page, when Arthur reassures Charles that everything will be all right, the words "the husband answered" are a late insertion that shows the wry attention to such categories ("the mother," "the spouse") that has been evident since the first page.

Writing is a matter of scorn to Arthur's son, and even Diana complains that she is "quite constipated with all the novels I read." By the end of the book, an artist's unnoticed juggling has been replaced with an act that never occurs: "The wrestling arena was dead empty, darkened." We can't know whether in this Henry Green consciously meant any comment on his own career. The novel's final words are "the next day they all went on very much the same." If with hindsight the irony relates not only to the book's characters, who badly need *not* to go on the same, but also to the novelist, we do not know how much intimation Henry himself had of this. Nor can we tell how Dig felt about the book's other themes and incidents: Arthur's midlife crisis; Diana's reiterations of the doctor's warnings against his drinking; the farce of her unexpected return to the apartment to find him washing a girl's dress after an accident with a coffee trolley; her near affair in retaliation; her scheming, her unhappiness, yet her unflagging dedication to her hopeless (in every sense) husband. Two things are certain, though. In *Doting*, more than in anything he had written before, Green depicted aspects of his marriage in a light very sympathetic to Dig. And it was the last book he wrote.

When it appeared in May 1952, it was a considerable success. Though some critics were disappointed at its artistic conservatism and what they took to be a lack of progress from the manner of *Nothing*, *Time and Tide* called it "the best so far" of his novels, and J. D. Scott in the *New Statesman* rightly described it as "witty, stylish, poignant, mordantly funny and horribly sad."[20] Leonard Woolf, who had already asked for an option on Henry's next book, was not surprised when *Doting* sold a comfortable 6,700 copies within ten months, bringing it close to the total figures by that date for *Concluding* (7,100) and *Nothing* (8,900).[21] In the States, meanwhile, though Green's sales never improved on the strong start made by *Loving*, *Nothing* had been a critical hit (Brendan Gill wrote in *The New Yorker*, "What the unprincipled fellow has gone and done is to write a funny book" that readers would enjoy "without once feeling a pang of conscience over the sorry state of the world"),[22] and *Concluding* had been picked by *Time* as one of three recent novels "that would be standouts in any year."[23] Meanwhile, Gallimard had bought the French rights to all of Green's novels (*Caught* had already appeared from Nagel in 1945 as *Orage sur Londres*).[24] And at home, the manuscript of *Loving* had been included in the exhibition *Modern Books and Writers,* organized for the Festival of Britain by the National Book League. Henry proudly took Maud, Dig, and Sebastian to the opening party at 7 Albemarle Street and, put out at being asked to pay for their sherry, went down the road to the Ritz and with unusual expansiveness bought several bottles of champagne instead.[25]

The contents of the exhibition are a revealing snapshot of what counted in 1951—and also of the atmosphere in which such accounting took place. In trying to catch the precise tone of writing like Green's, one can easily forget how ponderous its verbal surroundings could be. The exhibition catalog describes the National Book League (NBL) as having been "entrusted by His Majesty's Government with the responsibility for the proper representation of books and literature in all Festival activities" and the NBL's mission as "the encouragement and appreciation of good reading matter clothed in seemly physical form."[26] The show was to answer the question "And what has Great Britain been up to in recent years?" an inquiry that was imagined as coming from someone "who had not seen a book for a quarter of a century"—as it might be, "a visitor from Greenland." Half of the exhibits were of book design, the other half—chosen by "Mr. V. S. Pritchett (in the Chair), Miss Rose Macaulay and Mr. (now Professor) C. Day Lewis"—were manuscripts representative of modern English writing, though "modern," the preface was quick to reassure readers, was used "without the slightest ulterior or *avant-gardiste* meaning."

Pritchett, Macaulay, and Day Lewis were, of course, serious writers—and they weren't responsible for this preface.[27] Their choice was interesting and eclectic: H. E. Bates, Max Beerbohm, Ronald Knox, Arthur Ransome, Bertrand Russell, and P. G. Wodehouse, as well as W. H. Auden, Elizabeth Bowen, Ivy Compton-Burnett, T. S. Eliot, Graham Greene, James Joyce, Katherine Mansfield, George Orwell, George Bernard Shaw, the Sitwells, Dylan Thomas, Virginia Woolf, W. B. Yeats, and others only a little less celebrated. The recently knighted Sir Maurice Bowra was included (perhaps he was in the selectors' minds when they wrote preemptively, "It sometimes happens that important books, especially of criticism, are badly written"). So were Robert Byron, Rosamond Lehmann, and Anthony Powell. Evelyn Waugh, who satirized the event as a piece of leftist "dreariness relieved by frivolity," devised what he called "A Progressive Game" in which you scored two points for each of the books you either possessed or had read, three if you could claim both, and claimed that Henry Green was the author who scored lowest in the reckoning of the people whom he had persuaded to play.[28]

This was a year before the publication of *Doting*, which, as it happened, coincided with the birth of Kitty's second daughter. To Henry's amusement, Kitty decided to call her Annabel ("it's lucky her surname isn't Paynton").[29] Despite his best efforts, he was still obsessed with her. After Poppet John's wedding two months earlier, Cyril Connolly's wife, Barbara Skelton, wrote in her diary that Henry had gone through "his usual repertoire," repeating everything that Kitty Freud said and bringing her name into every conversation.[30] Unable to visit her at the Royal Free Hospital because she had caught mumps and was kept in isolation, he sent her a flood of newsy letters. He and Dig were off to the Isle of Wight, he told her, to stay with their niece Josephine Lowry-Corry and her father, Montagu—whose mother Henry called his "ex mother-in-law," as if he had once been married to Miss.[31] A few days later, Josephine was off to Rome to see a boyfriend, and Henry had to go to Birmingham.[32] Sebastian, he related, had joined the Intelligence Corps, whose instructors surprised him by carrying on like marine sergeants, saying, "What we want in this unit is bags of GUTS." Henry gave full details of the imminent *Life* magazine interview but said, "Promise not to read the thing if it's printed, it's too bogus."

Meanwhile, there were more than the usual frustrations at Pontifex. On Goronwy Rees's advice, the company had decided to sell and lease back the George Street headquarters, but the money due was delayed: "I'm in a state of rage and confusion and of course our solicitor is in his Bentley on the Riviera. I could kill all these bloody crooks."[33] The matter preoccupied him so much that it had even made him forget Kitty "for one hour and ten minutes. How are you darling?" Kitty softened enough under this barrage to suggest a rendezvous as soon as she got out of the hospital, when she went to stay at her in-laws' house at Walberswick in Suffolk. But events frustrated them in the farcical way that Henry always partly relished. All the hotels in Southwold were full. Through contacts in the brewery trade, he managed to find a single room in a pub and made the complicated journey by train and bus (he had never learned to drive), only to discover that Lucian had chosen that day to come see Kitty and the children.[34]

It was some time before the chastened Henry was in touch with Kitty again. In the spring of 1953, she brought her daughters to see him, and he wrote to her afterward, vividly recalling Annie, "those eyelashes as thick as black cropped grass. And her black rogue's eyes—the way she holds one's hand very tight and how she laughs with your special mockery when she allows one to pick her up. I love every centimetre of her and she reminds me of you." Then he remembered himself and apologized: "Forgive this—don't worry, I'm not going to be much of a nuisance."[35]

But it was to himself that he was being a nuisance, more than to Kitty. That spring, she met and fell in love with a young musician of her own age. Wynne Godley, the younger son of an Irish peer, was a professional oboist and also a brilliant economist in the making. Henry found it hard to conceal his jealousy, especially when Kitty told him—intending it as a compliment—that she had lent Wynne copies of Henry's books: "Now sooner or later I'll be told what he thinks of them and out of politeness to you I'll have to hold my tongue."[36] Gradually, though, Henry reconciled himself to the inevitable, writing to her more cheerfully three months later from Venice, where he and Dig were sent by British *Vogue*.

Foreign travel had only recently opened up again, and the Yorkes did all the usual things, visiting Torcello, eating a lot, and trying to avoid bumping into other English people.[37] Henry found the language ridiculous but everything else beautiful except the girls. His spirits lifted enough for him to venture a joke about "hideous demonic orgies" between Kitty and Wynne in County Clare, and by the following year he was able to write to her warmly about her impending marriage: "I hope and am sure the sun will always shine on you in your new life. . . . I don't know anyone who deserves more good things than you do."[38] Both he and Dig had already made friends with Wynne, and the two couples were to remain close for the rest of Henry's life.

In December 1952, Kitty was alone with her children and about to go into the hospital for a sinus operation, Dig was suffering the aftereffects of some painful dentistry, Maud was also out of sorts, and Henry found himself doing an unusual amount of fetching and carrying. He also exerted himself on behalf of John Lehmann. When Lehmann left the

Hogarth Press, he had set up a publishing house in his own name, in partnership with a firm of printers, Purnell. The project had been discouraged by Lehmann's friends, Blanche Knopf among them, who thought he would be better suited to working as the salaried literary adviser of a well-established house, but he had wanted freedom and adventure. His distinguished list included important American work such as Saul Bellow's *Dangling Man* (which Leonard Woolf had turned down) and Paul Bowles's *The Sheltering Sky;* a number of European poets in translation; a series of forgotten or unpublished works by classic authors, including Stendhal's two-volume unfinished *Lucien Leuwen;* and first novels by aspiring English writers such as the Yorkshire miner, Percy Coates. None of these had exactly become a bestseller, but Lehmann resisted with horror warnings from Purnell, which owned 51 percent of the business, about the need for profitability. In December 1952, the printer decided to close him down. Once set in action, the process was carried out with some ruthlessness, though Purnell may not have been as cruel as Lehmann thought in rejecting a last-minute low offer from the young Robert Maxwell, to whom Lehmann had taken a shine.

The literary world can be friendlier to failure than it is often thought to be—though perhaps it is partly a case of there being no pleasure keener than seeing your neighbor fall off his roof.[39] Lehmann was buoyed up by expressions of sympathy.[40] Perhaps to appease his conscience about not having stayed with Lehmann when he left Hogarth, Henry took it on himself to arrange what he exaggeratedly described as "the first occasion authors have given one of their own kind a *meal* since Coleridge organized a dinner for Leigh Hunt on his release from prison."[41] Characteristically, he asked each of the guests to send payment in advance. Anthony Powell and Philip Toynbee complained about the price (a steep 18s 6d, drinks not included) but paid up.[42] Cecil Day Lewis declined because Rosamond Lehmann was bound to be there, Elizabeth Bowen because she was going to be in the States. The Cambridge don "Dadie" Rylands, who had been among Lehmann's predecessors as the Woolfs' assistant at the Hogarth Press, sent the most colorful of the replies:

> Of course if dear John Lehmann has done so much for all of you
> I am delighted to help give him a LUNCH. I remember for many

years "doing so much for him" when he came up from Eton and began to compose poems and edit undergraduate mags—and that was only the beginning of what had to be done. . . . Do you want me to send 18/6 to Pontifex Maximus *before* I know the date and irrespective of whether I can sit with all the younger poets, novelists, soundings, ex-beauties. Will the Navy be represented?

The lunch eventually took place in a private room at the Trocadero on Piccadilly Circus. Stephen Spender was to find to his surprise that it was "really . . . not at all boring."[43] Koestler arrived late and had to sit at a table of people "all of whom hated him." Connolly made a scene about the wine, alleging that when he asked the waiter for the best on the list, he must have been misheard as asking for the worst. Otherwise, as Spender continued with enjoyable malice,

> everyone behaved as though he was being consciously at once disappointed and a disappointment. The speeches reinforced this impression. Henry Green got up and said that when he began to arrange this meal, forty-nine (I think) people were invited and of these, much to his surprise, thirty-seven accepted. If there were only thirty-two present, this was because five had suddenly been struck down by flu. He thought it was a jolly good show, and a surprising tribute to John Lehmann. With this he sat down. Then Eliot got up, looking bowed and old, leaning forward with his hands on the tablecloth and staring down at the table. With infinite gravity he said that he shared three occupations . . . or should he say professions? . . . with John Lehmann: as poet, businessman and publisher. He was quite sure that whatever happened . . . and he didn't have any air of knowing in particular what would happen . . . John would carry on with one of these. Then he sat down. John then got up and said he didn't know what to say . . . (always a good beginning). . . . As an editor he always had a feeling of being haunted: he was haunted by articles, stories and poems which flooded in on him, haunted by ideas or articles and poems suggested to him. He also had to send out a great many rejection slips, by the consciousness of

which he was haunted also. (We all shuddered, Cyril putting on an expression as though he were stuffed with John's rejection slips.) . . . His speech ended with a peroration in which he managed to introduce the names of most of Henry Green's novels. He didn't want us to think, he said, that he was going to "pack his bag." He wanted to assure Mr Green that he intended to go on *living* and that he thanked him for his *loving* if not his *doting* care. There would be no turning *back*, etc.

One of those who missed the lugubrious fun was the poet Norman Nicholson. Before Christmas, he had written to Green from Cumberland explaining that "London in winter is about as accessible to me as the North Pole." With unconscious irony, he added, "I count you among the very very few contemporary writers of fiction to whose new work I look forward with continuing excitement."

CHAPTER 11

Young Fellows with Flashing Heels

EVERYONE WAS SAYING THAT A NEW LITERARY GEN-
eration was bound to emerge and that its values, like those of the rest of
British society, would be different: "meritocratic"; plainspokenly opposed to what it saw as pretension and obfuscation; opposed, too, to the
concentration of power—literary power not least—among Old Etonians.
True, Cyril Connolly was now the main book reviewer of *The Sunday
Times;* Alan Pryce-Jones was editor of the *TLS;* Anthony Powell was
running the books section of *Punch;* and John Lehmann was busy making book programs for the BBC. But in the meantime, Philip Larkin's
novels *Jill* and *A Girl in Winter* had appeared, and Kingsley Amis had
begun to establish himself as a writer.[1] By the mid-1950s, they and others
like them—well educated at grammar schools but from defiantly less
privileged provincial or suburban backgrounds—had come to be seen as
representing what was most promising in British writing. John Wain's
Hurry on Down appeared in 1953, Amis's *Lucky Jim* in 1954, Larkin's
The Less Deceived in 1955, John Osborne's *Look Back in Anger* in
1956, John Braine's *Room at the Top* in 1957.

As the poet and critic Julian Symons—an early sympathizer with
"The Movement" and among Henry Green's sternest critics—was to
write, "this battle of players against gentlemen, puritans against hedo-
nists, Goths against silver-age Romans, is a permanent one in twentieth-
century Britain."[2] Inevitably, the patterns detected subsequently by

ment came when the large London-made coffin was to be lowered close to where Vincent and the long-dead Philip lay. By mistake, a large stone had been left protruding into the side of the grave, and the coffin stuck firmly. It was an appropriate end for the man whose relish in the bizarre was to be recalled by V. S. Pritchett at his memorial service. "Swear to tell me," Henry had begged him once when he was going to a wedding, "everything that goes wrong."[44]

For a list of Green's publications, see the Select Bibliography. The following short titles are used in the notes:

PG	*Party Going* (London: Hogarth Press, 1939)
PMB	*Pack My Bag* (London: Hogarth Press, 1940)
Surviving	*Surviving: The Uncollected Writings of Henry Green,* ed. Matthew Yorke (London: Chatto and Windus, 1992)

In the notes, "HY" means Henry Yorke. Other sources frequently referred to are abbreviated as follows:

BBC	BBC Written Archive, Caversham
EC	Eton College Library (Nevill Coghill papers)
GEC	*The Complete Peerage; or, a History of the House of Lords and Its Members from the Earliest Times,* by G.E.C., 1998 edition
Hogarth	Archive of the Hogarth Press, Reading University Library
HR	Harry Ransom Humanities Research Center, University of Texas at Austin (papers of Edward Garnett, John Lehmann, Lady Ottoline Morrell, and other collections)
JY	Private archive of John Yorke
KG	Letters in the possession of Kitty Godley
King's	The Modern Archive of King's College Library, Cambridge (papers of Rosamond Lehmann)

Lucy Butler   Private archive of Lucy Butler (includes copies of letters from Robert Byron to others)

MK   Originals or copies of Mary Keene papers in the possession of Alice Keene

NC   Library of the University of North Carolina at Chapel Hill, Manuscripts Department (J. M. Dent and Son Records)

Paul Bailey   Notes made by Paul Bailey while researching his projected biography

Princ   Firestone Library, Princeton University, Department of Rare Books and Special Collections (papers of John Lehmann)

Smith   Originals or copies of Matthew Smith papers in the possession of Alice Keene

SY   Private archive of Sebastian Yorke (includes copies of letters from Henry Green to others)

Unless otherwise stated, "interview" means a taped interview between the author and the person named.

Paul Bailey	21 September and 28 October 1993
Sir Isaiah Berlin	9 October 1991
Lucy Butler	8 October 1993 and 15 September 1998
Sir Raymond and Lady Carr	31 August 1994
Kitty Godley	24 September and 24 December 1997 and 18 August 1998
Reginald Hawkes	31 August 1994
Hidé Ishiguro	13 August 1992
Gerard Keenan	11 August 1998
Alice Keene	10 September 1991 and 6 January and 26 November 1993
Venetia Murray	6 April 1998
Conan Nicholas	12 July 1994
Pamela Nicholas	30 June 1994
Anthony Powell	23 November 1992 and 19 December 1994
Alan Pryce-Jones	6 June 1996

Jenny Rees	29 December 1994
Alan Ross	7 January 1993, 15 December 1994, and 13 January 1997
Mary Sanger-Davies	18 May 1994
Carol Southern	23 September 1997
Terry Southern	13–14 April 1991
Sir Stephen Spender	5 February 1994
Emma Tennant	25 May 1995
Eudora Welty	7 May 1992
John Yorke	31 July 1994 and 16 October 1998

In addition, I had a recorded conversation with Sebastian Yorke on 8 November 1992.

NOTES

PREFACE AND ACKNOWLEDGMENTS

1. Goronwy Rees, for example: see Ann Hancock, "The Life of Henry Yorke and the Writing of Henry Green" (Ph.D. diss., University of Warwick, 1981), 1.
2. *Surviving,* 179.

CHAPTER ONE: *Names*

1. *PMB,* 52, 56.
2. Eudora Welty, "Henry Green: A Novelist of the Imagination," *Texas Quarterly* 4 (1961): 246.
3. Wood also calls Lawrence, Woolf, and Green "the last serious European modernists." James Wood, *The Broken Estate: Essays on Literature and Belief* (London: Jonathan Cape, 1999), 186.
4. Introduction to *Surviving,* xvii.
5. Address delivered at Green's memorial service in Saint Paul's Knightsbridge, Wilton Place, 12 February 1974. A version was printed in *London Magazine* 14:2 (June–July 1974): 28f.
6. Welty, "Henry Green," 246.
7. Unpublished paper written for the M.A. requirement at Columbia University, ca. 1950; private communication from the author. The catalog of golden opinions could be very long indeed, but it is worth mentioning the opinion of Green's American contemporary, the novelist W. M. Spackman (1905–1990), that "Green is of course more gifted than [Henry] James." *The New Yorker,* 4 August 1997, 72.
8. HY to John Lehmann, 24 January 1941 (HR).
9. Geoffrey Scott, *The Portrait of Zélide* (London: Constable, 1925).
10. Harold Acton, *Memoirs of an Aesthete* (London: Methuen, 1948), 93.
11. In 1883, he ranked tenth in terms of income among the English nobility and was twenty-fourth in order of acreage owned (*GEC*).

12. Lord Egremont, *Wyndham and Children First* (London: Macmillan, 1968), 61.

13. *PMB,* 7. Gerald Yorke confirmed the story in the annotations to his copy, which is still at Forthampton. Henry had given his mother the opportunity to object to "any purely family reference" in a final draft. She made one or two factual corrections: Her dog was a spaniel not a retriever; the Australian soldier mentioned was a Canadian. Henry ignored both points but at her request did moderate his comments on his Eton housemaster. Hancock, "The Life of Henry Yorke," 59–60.

14. *Surviving,* 14f.

15. *PMB,* 14. For other descriptions of Maud Yorke, I have relied on Sebastian Yorke's introductions to *Surviving* and to the 1992 Hogarth Press reissue of *PMB;* Maurice Bowra's *Memories, 1898–1939* (Cambridge, Mass.: Harvard University Press, 1966), 164–65; and both an interview with Anthony Powell and his *Infants of the Spring* (London: Heinemann, 1976), 66.

16. *PMB,* 24.

17. John Russell, "There It Is," *Kenyon Review* 26 (1964): 441.

18. *Blindness,* 213–14.

19. Bowra, *Memories, 1898–1939,* 165.

20. *Blindness,* 47.

21. Ibid.

22. Robert Byron, *Letters Home,* ed. Lucy Butler (London: Murray, 1991), 10. This was in February 1922, when Henry was sixteen. Byron's characteristic comment on Lord Leconfield's dog-in-the-mangerism was "so sensible, I think."

23. Interview with Anthony Powell.

24. For example, John's stepmother calls his father Ralph on pp. 41, 46, and 62 of *Blindness,* but in the nanny's thoughts on pp. 109 and 173, John's mother is called Mrs. Richard Haye.

25. All of the first earl's children did well: Philip Yorke became the second earl (see below); Charles became attorney general; Joseph (see p. 265, n. 30) a diplomat; John a lawyer and politician. Elizabeth and Margaret both married rich men. See David Souden, *Wimpole Hall, Cambridgeshire* (London: National Trust, 1991), 25–26. Souden quotes a harsh verdict on the Yorkes by Horace Walpole (son of Hardwicke's Whig opponent Robert Walpole), who spoke of the "miserable and pernicious turn of the whole family, than which nothing can be more illiberal and wretched, though possessed of immense wealth and the children matched into the most wealthy families," 19.

26. See p. 156.

27. *PMB,* 13.

28. Sebastian Yorke in *Surviving,* 286–87.

29. See Merlin Waterson, *The Servants' Hall: A Domestic History of Erddig* (London: Rutledge and Kegan Paul, 1980). The Yorkes of Erddig were descended from Simon Yorke, uncle of the first Lord Hardwicke. It was Simon's son, Philip (1743–1804), who began the practice, which was kept up without interruption into the twentieth century by a family whose staff members were often children of servants at Erddig. The pictures and verses can still be seen at the house, which now belongs to the National Trust.

30. Since Vincent Yorke's time, Isabelle de Charrière's books have gained a new readership, partly as a result of feminist literary criticism. But she was always known to English readers, and in 1925, when Green completed *Blindness,* an English biography appeared, Geoffrey Scott's *The Portrait of Zélide,* along with translations of several of her books. When "Belle" was in her early twenties, she met two British men at The Hague. One was the British ambassador, who as it happens was Joseph Yorke, brother of the bishop. He gave a ball to celebrate George III's birthday, at which Belle was one of the guests. The other was James Boswell, with whom she had a famous romance, which her most recent biographer, C. P. Courtney, has described as "essentially an encounter between two young writers in search of their identity, each of whom has a particular way of looking at reality—and distorting it." Both, Courtney continues, "had mobile temperaments and both complained of fits of depression which would . . . give way to wild gaiety." What they had most in common was that "they were compulsive writers and wrote mainly about themselves." They were secretive about these personal writings, Boswell about his diary, Belle about her clandestine letters, whether written to him or to the numerous other men to whom she became close. In these respects as in others, Belle de Zuylen's character was to be echoed in that of Henry Yorke. Each had an early interest in the poor while remaining essentially conservative in outlook. Each started writing young: Belle's *Le Noble,* an autobiographical satire on a pedigree-obsessed father who refuses to allow his daughter to make an "unsuitable" marriage, appeared when she was twenty-three; Henry Green's *Blindness* when he was twenty-one. And when they were still only in their late forties, both were to retreat into near seclusion at home, finding there not happiness by any means but something less unmanageable than in the wider social world, where as young people each could appear to be so easy. See C. P. Courtney, *Isabelle de Charrière (Belle de Zuylen): A Biography* (Oxford: Voltaire Foundation, 1993), 93.

31. Brian Masters, *The Life of E. F. Benson* (London: Chatto and Windus, 1991), 85–86.

32. For public information on Vincent Yorke, I have mainly relied on the long obituary of him published in the King's College, Cambridge, *Annual Report,* 1958, 18f., and on his entries in successive editions of *Who's Who.*

33. *PMB,* 69.

34. Real (in the sense of "royal") tennis originated in medieval France. It is a cross between handball and modern tennis.

35. See *PMB,* 11. Wright's *English Dialect Dictionary* is still among the books at Forthampton. For Henry's ease with Vincent, see Powell, *Infants of the Spring,* 67.

36. Paul Bailey, interview with Gerald Yorke, unpublished.

37. Quoted by Hancock, "The Life of Henry Yorke," 21.

38. Sebastian Yorke in *Surviving,* 287.

39. Interview with Anthony Powell.

40. *PMB,* 19.

41. Conversation with Sebastian Yorke.

42. See pp. 171–72.

43. I am grateful to Mary Sanger-Davies and George Wells for their memories of the village at this time.

44. *PMB,* 11, 13.

45. Lord Berners, *A Distant Prospect* (London: Constable, 1945), 96–97.

46. In revenge for having been kicked by the vicar's donkey, Cerberus once sank his teeth into the donkey's nose. Vincent had to throw a bucket of water over him before he would let go. Letter from George Wells.

47. F. M. L. Thompson, in *English Landed Society in the Nineteenth Century* (London: Routledge and Kegan Paul, 1963), shows how heavily involved old money had been with new since the industrial revolution.

48. Dorothy Yorke told Lucy Butler a story about an occasion when she was in charge of a picnic for the young princes at Balmoral. Having helped drag an unusually heavy hamper up a hill to the picnic spot, she opened it to find that they would be eating off gold plate.

49. See above, n. 32.

50. Forthampton Court now has about three thousand acres, two thousand rented out and one thousand "in hand." These figures were not, though, large by the standards of the Yorkes' world. In 1883, Maud's father owned sixty-six thousand acres in England and forty-four thousand in Ireland (*GEC*). As late as 1933, Lord Wemyss, grandfather of Henry's close friend and neighbor Mary Strickland, recorded with nonchalant precision in *Who's Who* that he owned "about 62,100 acres."

51. Berners, *Distant Prospect,* 65.

52. *GEC; Who's Who.*

53. *PMB,* 64f. A plaque behind the old front door at Forthampton Court records that 104 men were treated there between 1 November 1917 and 1 February 1919.

54. Ibid., 69.

55. Ibid., 67. This man had come to Forthampton before the nursing home had

been set up. Henry remembered him as Australian, but he was a Canadian. *PMB,* 66; Hancock, "The Life of Henry Yorke," 60.

56. Egerton's, 13 Somerset Street, Portman Square. In the summer of 1913, he placed eleventh out of twelve boys for the term's work. He did better on average in the exams, coming in sixth, despite conspicuously poor performances in English (on which he scored a 13 out of a possible 50) and elementary science (16/50). Under "Writing and Dictation," his report for the term described him as "Careful and promising," but for English the comment was "Must try & answer better" and for "Reading and Repetition," "must try and recite with more expression." Maud Yorke's scrapbook at Forthampton (JY).

57. *PMB,* 86.

58. Maud Yorke's scrapbook at Forthampton (JY).

59. Powell, *Infants of the Spring,* 67.

60. Ibid.

61. See Stanley Jackson, *The Sassoons* (London: Heinemann, 1968).

62. *PMB,* 47. As usual, the uncle is not named, but he was identified by Gerald Yorke in one of his marginal notes (see above, n. 13).

63. These and other details about New Beacon are taken from a series of articles about the school by C. L. Norman, published in the school magazine, *The Beacon,* October 1963–October 1969.

64. *PMB,* 42. Knole had been the childhood home of Vita Sackville-West. Married to Harold Nicolson by the time Henry was at New Beacon, she still often stayed at the house with her father, Lord Sackville. Her situation as an aristocratic author intrigued her future friend and lover Virginia Woolf, who explored it in *Orlando*—published two years after *Blindness.* Woolf believed, or thought she believed, that "no aristocrat can write a book" because "it is from the middle class that writers spring." See Sandra M. Gilbert's notes to *Orlando,* ed. Brenda Lyons (Harmondsworth: Penguin, 1993), 242.

65. Most of the details in this and the following paragraph come from *PMB,* esp. pp. 20–26, 36–37, and 76–80.

66. Powell, *Infants of the Spring,* 64.

67. *PMB,* 27–28.

68. Ibid., 22.

69. Paul Bailey, interview with Gerald Yorke, unpublished; Sebastian Yorke in *Surviving,* 296.

70. *PMB,* 46, 25–26.

71. Ibid., 43, 36–37. Anthony Powell remembers Henry as "the least queer person you've ever met."

72. *Grand Street* 42 (1992): 42–45.

73. *PMB,* 19.

74. Ibid., 18.

CHAPTER TWO: *Society of Arts*

1. *The Eton Register,* part 8, 1909–1919, compiled for the Old Etonian Association, 1932.
2. Danny Danziger, ed., *Eton Voices* (London: Viking, 1988), 123.
3. Such was the future Lord Home's dedication to Eton that he married the headmaster's daughter. Henry Green commented, "Anyone who marries his headmaster's daughter has touched wood, don't you agree?" Russell, "There It Is," 457.
4. *PMB,* 98.
5. Danziger, *Eton Voices,* 181.
6. *PMB,* 93.
7. Interview with Alan Pryce-Jones. In his autobiography, Pryce-Jones says that his friend's only piece was a version of Mendelssohn's "On Wings of Song," which he played "a constant quarter-tone flat." *The Bonus of Laughter* (London: H. Hamilton, 1987), 27.
8. *PMB,* 167. "Appropriately enough," like "characteristically," was a phrase Green often used in self-disparaging contexts. Cf. *PMB,* 142, 154.
9. Brian Howard, quoted in Martin Green, *Children of the Sun: A Narrative of "Decadence" in England after 1918* (London: Constable, 1977), 118.
10. *PMB,* 85, 27.
11. Ibid., 152–53.
12. 1,157 Old Etonians were killed in the First World War, a fifth of all those from the school who fought. Tim Card, *Eton Renewed* (London: J. Murray, 1994), 142.
13. Paul Bailey, interview with Gerald Yorke, unpublished.
14. *PMB,* 108.
15. HY to Nevill Coghill, 10 April 1926 (EC).
16. *PMB,* 101.
17. Ibid., 100.
18. Ibid., 98.
19. Interview with Alan Pryce-Jones.
20. Fives is a form of handball. Eton has its own version of the game.
21. *PMB,* 160.
22. Byron, *Letters Home,* 8.
23. Ibid., 11.
24. Unpublished portion of ibid., March 1922 (Lucy Butler).
25. Green, *Children of the Sun,* 115.
26. Acton, *Memoirs of an Aesthete,* 80.
27. Robert Byron to HY, 21 March 1923 (Lucy Butler).
28. HY at Eton to Maud Yorke, n.d. (SY).
29. For Byron's involvement in the resignation see *Letters Home,* 10–15. Byron

had made a name for himself in the corps by taking an umbrella on parade and opening it at the onset of rain.

30. Prior to the First World War, as many as 50 percent of the boys did not join the corps. Card, *Eton Renewed,* 142.

31. Henry wrote to his mother that Whitworth "is very stupid, I don't think he has the slightest idea of how to treat boys." HY at Eton to Maud Yorke, 3 October [year unknown] (SY).

32. Housemaster's report dated 19 December 1922 (SY).

33. Interview with Anthony Powell.

34. Green, *Children of the Sun,* 174.

35. See below, chap. 5. Bryan Guinness and Henry Yorke were born within two days of each other, the former on 27 October 1905.

36. Pryce-Jones's *Private Opinion* (London: Cobden-Sanderson, 1936), is sub-titled *A Commonplace Book* and was intended as "an indirect and imper-sonal autobiography," but, as the author admits in the introduction, "In the end . . . Egotism crept in."

37. Anthony Powell's four volumes of memoirs, collectively titled *To Keep the Ball Rolling,* appeared in 1976–1982. His story is continued in a series of journals that began to appear in 1995.

38. Acton, *Memoirs of an Aesthete,* 98.

39. *PMB,* 166.

40. Marie-Jacqueline Lancaster, ed., *Brian Howard: Portrait of a Failure* (Lon-don: Blond, 1968), 121. The libretto was by Alan Clutton-Brock, the scenery by Colin Anderson.

41. "I had to play in M'Tutor's jazzband which consists of one piano, two swanee whistles, 1 swanee piccolo, 1 banjo, 1 violin and me—who plays drum cym-bal bell hollow box all with two drumsticks. We really are very good. Henry comes sometimes plus fiddle." Byron, *Letters Home,* 16.

42. Acton, *Memoirs of an Aesthete,* 93.

43. *Blindness,* 3. Throughout his life this remained his view of one of the roles of writing. See pp. 62, 207.

44. *PMB,* 165.

45. *College Days,* no. 8, 17 March 1923, 246–47. It has never been reprinted.

46. "Bees" is reprinted in *Surviving,* 3–5. Among the features the village has in common with Forthampton are its almshouses close to the graveyard. The Reverend Hugh Sanger-Davies came to Forthampton as vicar in 1918, having previously been curate at the Bristol parishes of Saint Thomas, Eastville, and Saint Anne, Greenbank.

47. Sanger-Davies himself was in fact a keen reader—so much so that when he re-tired his parishioners gave him a revolving bookcase. (Interview with his daughter, Mary Sanger-Davies.)

48. Letter in family scrapbook at Forthampton (JY). In his afterword to *Surviv-*

ing, Sebastian Yorke writes: "Early stories were shown to John Buchan who strongly advised him to give it all up as a bad job" (*Surviving,* 291). Henry himself seems to have thought that it was *Blindness* that Buchan discouraged (ibid., 133).

49. Typescript draft of *Blindness* entitled "Progression," 71–72 (SY). The other Everyman volumes listed are: *Mansfield Park, Pilgrim's Progress,* Browning's *Poems,* Carlyle's *French Revolution,* William Canton's *The Invisible Playmate, The Mill on the Floss,* Gogol's *Dead Souls* and *Taras Bulba and Other Stories,* and W. F. Kirkby's *Kalevala.*

50. The full list of "miscellaneous volumes" consists of: Addison's *Essays,* Beckford's *Vathek,* Blake's *Poems,* Carew's *Poems,* G. K. Chesterton's *Heretics and Orthodoxy,* Congreve's *Incognita,* Goldsworthy Lowes Dickinson's *A Modern Symposium,* Anatole France's *My Friend's Book* and *The Garden of Epicurus,* John Gay's *Poems,* Robert Herrick's *Poems,* Longus's *Daphnis and Chloe,* Katherine Mansfield's *The Dove's Nest and Others, The Garden Party,* and *Bliss,* George Moore's *Esther Waters, Hail and Farewell, Lewis Seymour and Some Women,* George Meredith's *Miscellaneous Prose,* Nashe's *The Unfortunate Traveller,* Matthew Prior's *Shorter Poems,* Ruskin's *Crown of Wild Olives* and *Time and Tide,* Schopenhauer's *The Art of Literature,* Spenser's *Faerie Queene,* book 1, and *Epithalamion,* Sterne's *Tristram Shandy,* Robert Louis Stevenson's *Inland Voyage* and *Dr. Jekyll and Mr. Hyde,* Swinburne's *Mary Stuart,* Vaughan's *Poems,* and Wilde's *De Profundis.*

51. *PMB,* 95.

52. "Unloving," *Surviving,* 280. See also *Infants of the Spring,* 105–6.

53. *Blindness,* 16.

54. *PMB,* 126.

55. Robert Byron in Austria to HY, n.d. [August 1928] (Lucy Butler).

56. In "Mood," Constance recalls walking across the deserted school yard at Eton and, when she hears the laugh of another girl, thinking joyfully, "Isn't that gorgeous in a place built in fear like this" (*Surviving,* 42).

57. The traveler and poet Wilfrid Scawen Blunt (1840–1922) was a nephew of George Wyndham, first Baron Leconfield.

58. Interview with her daughter, Sara Carr.

59. *PMB,* 173ff. As so often, his memories here were also caught up in the present in which he was writing. See p. 240.

60. The episode was reenacted in the 1992 BBC-TV documentary *Trapped: The Story of Henry Green,* directed by Roger Thompson.

61. *PMB,* 120.

62. "I began to write a novel. I began to meet girls." Ibid., 172.

63. In *Infants of the Spring,* 106–7, Anthony Powell warns against taking Green's account of these days in *PMB* at face value, pointing out that readers would

never guess from the book that he was "a gifted witty companion." Powell had particular reason to be alert to his friend's attractiveness to women: See pp. 71–72.

64. Byron, *Letters Home*, 9–10.
65. *The Times* (London), 27 and 28 February 1923; *PMB*, 145–52.
66. *PMB*, 146.
67. Green refers to his grandmother rather than grandparents. Both Yorke grandparents were still alive, but Maud's father had died in 1901.

CHAPTER THREE: *Drinking Through a Straw*

1. *PMB*, 185.
2. Ibid.
3. In *Classes and Cultures: England, 1918–1951* (Oxford: Oxford University Press, 1998), Ross McKibbin writes interestingly about the demographics of different sports and entertainments, mentioning "sporting bohemianism" as a phenomenon that "harmlessly satisfied democratic impulses" among a "handful of high-born persons" in this period (362).
4. Letter in family scrapbook at Forthampton, 18 July 1925 (JY).
5. HY to Maud Yorke, n.d. (SY).
6. *PMB*, 188.
7. Ibid., 200, 202.
8. Robert Byron's father was another exception, "furious with [him] for only getting a Third" (letter to the author from Lucy Butler).
9. Information from the archivist of Magdalen College, Oxford.
10. Postcard from HY at Magdalen to Coghill, n.d.: "I am desperate. The novel is stuck in a quagmire. I have come to the end of every idea. And Simpson makes one work 8 hours a day. Very agreeable work, but it cements my brain up with archaisms" (EC).
11. A. N. Wilson, *C. S. Lewis: A Biography* (London: Collins, 1990), 98.
12. Bowra, *Memories,* 163. Henry cared enough about Anglo-Saxon poetry to show his rendering of the poem "Judith" to Coghill (SY).
13. Henry asked his mother for the complete works of Dostoevsky, Gorky, and Moore as his Christmas present in 1925 (SY).
14. HY to Maud Yorke, 8 November 1926 (SY).
15. The match was played at Eyeles's Rooms, Oxford, on 10 and 11 March 1926. Yorke was second string, scoring 403 to the 387 of C. H. M. Millar (Queen's College) and the 346 of C. E. Frazer (Balliol). *Oxford versus Cambridge: A Record of Inter-university Contests from 1827–1930*, ed. H. M. Abrahams and J. Bruce Kerr (London: Faber and Faber, 1931), 80.
16. *PMB*, 217.

17. Ibid., 201.

18. Byron, *Letters Home,* 53, 6 November 1925.

19. Quoted in Lancaster, *Brian Howard,* 212.

20. Evelyn Waugh, *A Little Learning* (London: Chapman and Hall, 1964), 213. Waugh first met "a freshman called Yorke" in November 1924 over lunch with Harold Acton. The other guests included William Lygon (Lord Elmley) and Robert Byron. Evelyn Waugh, *The Diaries of Evelyn Waugh,* ed. Michael Davie (London: Weidenfeld and Nicolson, 1976), 18 November 1924.

21. Powell, *Infants of the Spring,* 185.

22. Byron, *Letters Home,* 11.

23. Audrey Field, *Picture Palace: A Social History of the Cinema* (London: Gentry Books, 1974), 66.

24. McKibbin, *Classes and Cultures,* 419.

25. Waugh, *Diaries,* 3 September 1924.

26. Dennis Sharp, *The Picture Palace and Other Buildings for the Movies* (New York: Praeger, 1969).

27. Early in Henry's first term, the university magazine *Isis* recommended the Scala as "the . . . one cinema we know where the front seats take a laudable and audible interest in the fortunes of the hero." *Isis,* 29 October 1924.

28. *Beau Brummell* was at the Oxford Super Cinema, 13–15 November 1924; *Cyrano* at the Electra, 2 February 1925; *Tess,* Electra, 23 February 1925; *David Copperfield,* Electra, 16 February 1925; *Pompeii,* Electra, 29 November 1926.

29. *Sahara,* Oxford Super Cinema, 6 October 1924; *Great White Silence,* George Street, 20 October 1924.

30. Reviewed in *Isis,* 12 November 1924.

31. The first Oxford film was *Silent,* produced by Hugh Brooke. It was shown at the Oxford Super Cinema in the week of 17 June 1926. The second, *Next Gentleman, Please,* produced by John Greenidge and Rudolph Messell, was shown starting 6 December, at the same theater.

32. *Living,* 59.

33. *Happiness,* Oxford Super Cinema, 27 October 1924; *Secrets,* New Cinema, Headington, 12 January 1925; *Rosita,* Oxford Super Cinema, 8 December 1924; *Zaza,* Electra, 9 February 1925; *Orphans,* Scala, 3 November 1924.

34. Powell, *Infants of the Spring,* 182.

35. Ibid., 188.

36. Waugh, *Diaries,* 325.

37. Bowra, *Memories,* 165.

38. Hugh Lloyd-Jones, ed., *Maurice Bowra: A Celebration* (London: Duckworth, 1974), 16f.

39. Ibid., 92.

40. *PMB*, 202–3.

41. "Eleven Occasional Poems: VII. Eulogy," in W. H. Auden, *Collected Poems,* ed. Edward Mendelson (London: Faber and Faber, 1976), 572. Henry Green's own description of the (unnamed) Coghill can be found in *PMB,* 204–5.

42. HY to Nevill Coghill, n.d. (EC).

43. Charles Doughty, *Adam Cast Forth* (London: Duckworth, 1908), 2.

44. Ibid., 46.

45. "So she stood in the ground-floor department of Messrs. Marshall & Snelgrove. . . . Then she got into the lift . . . and was shot smoothly upwards. The very fabric of life now, she thought as she rose, is magic. . . . 'When I step out of doors—as I do now,' here she stepped on to the pavement of Oxford Street, 'what is it that I taste? Little herbs. I hear goat bells. I see mountains. . . .' Her eyes filled with tears." *Orlando* (1928), 207, 210.

46. HY to Coghill, postmarked 26 March 1925 (EC).

47. Ibid., n.d. (EC). The letter is headed "8 King Edward Street," so it dates from Henry's second or third year at Oxford.

48. Ibid., postmarked 26 March 1925 (EC).

49. Ibid., n.d. (EC).

50. Ibid., 18 December 1926 (EC).

51. HY at Magdalen to Coghill, n.d. (EC).

52. Nevill Coghill at Exeter College, Oxford, to HY, 24 March 1925 (EC).

53. HY to Coghill, 8 April [1925] (EC).

54. Notebook entries cited by Russell, "There It Is," 444.

55. HY to Coghill, 8 April [1925] (EC).

56. "Arcady," *Surviving,* 27.

57. Hancock, "The Life of Henry Yorke," 35.

58. Chatto and Windus archives, Reading University Library. The Manuscripts Entry Book for 1925 records that the parcel arrived on 27 June.

59. Ibid., letter dated 22 July 1925.

60. HY to Coghill, n.d. (EC).

61. Pocock succeeded R. Wilson as Dent's educational adviser and editor in the summer of 1924. J. M. Dent, *The House of Dent, 1888–1938* (London: J. M. Dent, 1938), 254.

62. At Anthony Powell's suggestion, the book was also sent to the Powells' family friend Thomas Balston at Duckworth (who later gave Powell his first publishing job), but it met with no success. Powell, *Messengers of Day* (London: Heinemann, 1978), 6.

63. The scores of books written, edited, or compiled by Guy Pocock include an abbreviated version of *Bevis* published in 1937.

64. Henry Green described the encounter in the *New Statesman,* 30 November 1950. The piece is reprinted in *Surviving,* 133–35.

65. Ibid., 135. Green is talking about Garnett's skill with dialogue and narrative, having suggested that his touch was less reliable in matters of characterization.

66. George Jefferson, "Green and Garnett," *London Magazine,* June 1978, 53–62.

67. Coghill to HY, n.d. (SY); HY to Coghill, 27 December 1925 (EC).

68. HY at Forthampton to Edward Garnett, 21 December 1925 (HR).

69. HY at Petworth to Garnett, n.d. (HR).

70. *Blindness,* 195. Rod Mengham suggests that a "composite idea involving optics and representation" runs through Green's work from *Blindness* on (*The Idiom of the Time* [Cambridge: Cambridge University Press, 1982], ix).

71. *The Times Higher Education Supplement,* 26 August 1977.

72. There are also links with Dostoevsky and Gogol, interestingly explored by Mengham, *Idiom of the Time,* 1, 3, 11–12.

73. Gerald Yorke's letter book, 19 October 1926 (JY).

74. Paul Bailey, interview with Gerald and Angela Yorke, unpublished.

75. E. F. Benson at Lamb House, Rye, Sussex, to Vincent Yorke, n.d. (JY).

76. Lady Ottoline's biographer Miranda Seymour dates Henry's first visit around 1926: *Ottoline Morrell: Life on the Grand Scale* (London: Hodder and Stoughton, 1992), 409.

77. HY to Philip Morrell, condoling with him on the death of Lady Ottoline, 22 April 1938 (SY).

78. Seymour, *Ottoline Morrell,* 316f.

79. Powell, *Infants of the Spring,* 186.

80. HY to Coghill, 3 July 1926 (EC).

81. Ibid., 19 April 1926 (EC).

82. He left Coghill a lighthearted note about the strike, asking whether he intended "to use a pick & be generally useful." On the stationery of Coghill's college, n.d. (EC).

83. For example, he responded to an invitation to a ball at Exeter College by telling Coghill "you know I dont dance and never have been able to, the fear of falling ruining any pleasure that I might take in the music." Ibid., 19 April 1926 (EC).

84. Powell, *Infants of the Spring,* 185.

85. "Adventure in a Room," *Surviving,* 8, 10.

86. HY from Magdalen to Coghill, n.d. (EC).

87. Bowra wrote to Henry, "I feel you need a word of congratulation on Tony's third. I had little idea that this was what you had worked for all these years. It will be interesting to hear his line on it" (SY).

88. *Europe in the Looking-Glass* (1926), was the account of a journey in which Byron "dashed across [the Continent] in a large and powerful touring car" (*The Times Literary Supplement* [TLS], 9 December 1926, 900). Henry de-

scribed the book as "brilliant" in a review for *Cherwell*—his only contribution to the undergraduate paper (Hancock, "The Life of Henry Yorke," 38).

89. Gerald Yorke letter book, October 1926 (JY).
90. HY from Mansfield Street to Coghill, n.d. (EC).
91. HY to Maud Yorke, 8 November 1926 (SY).
92. HY to Vincent Yorke, 11 November 1926 (SY).
93. Coghill to HY, 15 December [1926]; replying to HY's of 12 December 1926 (SY).

CHAPTER FOUR: *Works*

1. HY to Maud Yorke, 9 January 1927 (SY).
2. *PMB*, 236–37.
3. HY to Coghill, 18 December 1926 (EC).
4. HY to Maud Yorke, 9 January 1927 (SY).
5. This was the view, for example, of Anthony Powell, who visited him there: *Messengers of Day*, 25.
6. HY from Farringdon Works to Coghill, 15 February 1927 (EC).
7. Henry told this to Bryan Guinness, who repeated it to Paul Bailey in a letter, 18 September 1980. Cf. the rural idiom of Tupe and Gates in *Living*, 98.
8. *PMB*, 239.
9. Information from Patrick Baird, Head of Service, Local Studies and History, Birmingham Central Library.
10. HY to Coghill, 15 February 1927 (EC).
11. HY to Vincent Yorke, 2 February 1927 (SY).
12. HY to Maud Yorke, 17 February 1927 (SY).
13. Julian Morrell to HY, n.d. (SY).
14. HY to Coghill, 8 October 1927 (EC).
15. HY to Maud Yorke, 9 and 23 January 1927 (SY).
16. HY to Mary Strickland, January 1928 (Paul Bailey).
17. *TLS*, 2 December 1926, 174. The reviewer was Margaret Marshall. Green and his publisher had waited impatiently for this verdict, Garnett writing to him on 16 November 1926, "I wonder how long that extremely cautious journal 'The Literary Supplement' will take to make up its 60 horsepower literary mind that the novel should be awarded one of its honorific certificates."
18. *The New Republic*, 29 December 1926, 174; *The Saturday Review of Literature*, 25 December 1926, 472. The U.S. publisher was Dutton.
19. Evelyn Waugh wrote to Henry, "It is extraordinary to me that anyone of our generation could have written so fine a book." In *The Letters of Evelyn Waugh*, ed. Mark Amory (London: Weidenfeld and Nicolson, 1980), 24. Robert Byron used *Blindness* as the peg for a piece in *Cherwell* about the Eton Society of Arts. See Hancock, "Life of Henry Yorke," 37.

20. HY to Coghill, 8 October 1927 (EC).

21. See *PMB*, 240–44.

22. *Surviving*, 66.

23. Bowra, *Memories*, 163.

24. Waugh, *Diaries*, 23 June 1930, 317. Waugh seems to have missed Green's satire at the expense of such aestheticism in *Living* (see p. 80).

25. Green's story "Saturday," for example, written at this time, is focused first on a pregnant woman, then on a couple whose child is ill. Much of *Living* concerns Mrs. Eames's maternalism and its influence on Lily's behavior, and there is also the memorable morning in the foundry when Arthur Jones bursts into song because "that night son had been born to him" (*Living*, 89–90).

26. See, for example, *Surviving*, 48, 53.

27. HY to Robert Byron, 10 February 1928 (Lucy Butler). "I want them to do a 3/6 edition . . . but it is very probable that they wont agree. . . . Dents have had the M.S.S. for close on 3 months now."

28. Ibid.

29. Byron, *Letters Home*, 96.

30. Edward Garnett to HY, 27 November 1927 (SY).

31. See pp. 88–90.

32. Anthony Powell to HY, postmarked 26 May 1927, postmarked 3 October 1927, 7 November 1927, and 27 November [unknown] (SY).

33. HY to Coghill, 8 October 1927 (EC).

34. Ibid.

35. HY to Anthony Powell, 11 April 1928 (SY). This was the period when Eliot's first wife, Vivienne, was in a succession of Continental asylums, and the desperate Eliot himself refused most invitations and "placed his new faith around him like a carapace" (Peter Ackroyd, *T. S. Eliot* [London: H. Hamilton, 1984], 168f.). Aldous Huxley's brother was the scientist Julian.

36. HY to Byron, 20 February 1928 (Lucy Butler).

37. HY to Anthony Powell, 23 August 1928 (SY).

38. *PMB*, 245.

39. Interview with Anthony Powell.

40. *Surviving*, 33.

41. Told by Dig Yorke to Paul Bailey.

42. Interview with Reginald Hawkes.

43. John Symonds, *The Great Beast: The Life and Magick of Aleister Crowley* (Saint Albans: Mayflower, 1971 [1952]), preface.

44. Ibid., 362, 380.

45. The first class was divided in those days. Gerald took a I:ii in part 1 in 1922 and a I:i in part 2 in 1923—the best degree of a year that included Michael Oakeshott. Information from the archivist of Cambridge University.

46. Interview with John Yorke; correspondence with Jonathan Smith, Manuscript Cataloguer, Trinity College, Cambridge.

47. HY to Powell, 29 December 1927 (SY). Rummel's first marriage, to Thérèse Chaigneau, had broken up after his affair with Isadora Duncan. He married Sarah Harrington shortly after the First World War and divorced her in 1930. Omar Pound and Robert Spoo, eds., *Ezra Pound and Margaret Cravens: A Tragic Friendship, 1910–1912* (Durham, N.C.: Duke University Press, 1988), 151–58. I am grateful to Warwick Gould and John Stokes for information about this episode.

48. Ibid.

49. HY to Maud Yorke, 28 March 1928 (SY).

50. HY to Vincent Yorke, 23 August 1928 (SY).

51. HY at the Roosevelt Hotel, New Orleans, to Anthony Powell, 11 April 1928 (SY).

52. HY at the Hotel Pennsylvania, New York, to Maud Yorke, n.d. [1928] (SY).

53. HY at the Roosevelt Hotel, New Orleans, to Anthony Powell, 11 April 1928 (SY).

54. Ibid. The episode was to be echoed in the opening pages of *Doting* (1952): "Once more the elder Middleton looked down [Miss Paynton's] dress, but, this time, his son caught him at it" (7). But by then Green also had in mind outings with his own embarrassed son.

55. HY to Margaret Byron, 29 October 1928 (Lucy Butler).

56. Robert Byron to HY, 29 May [1928?] (Lucy Butler).

57. *Living*, 170.

58. At 36 Lowndes Street (JY).

59. HY to Maud Yorke, 8 September 1928 (SY).

60. Ibid., 24 August 1928 (SY).

61. HY to Anthony Powell, 23 August 1928 (SY).

62. HY to Maud Yorke, 18 September 1928 (SY).

63. Ibid., 24 August 1928 (SY).

64. It took place on 27 June 1928.

65. W. H. Auden to HY, 12 March and 18 August 1928 (SY).

66. Martin Stannard, *Evelyn Waugh* (London: Paladin 1988–1992), 1:158. The Guinness wedding took place in January 1929 (see Harold Acton, *Nancy Mitford: A Memoir* [London: H. Hamilton, 1975], 26).

67. Powell, *Messengers of Day*, 199.

68. HY to Maud Yorke, 18 September 1928 (SY). The visit was planned for 19 October.

69. Pansy Pakenham, sister of Frank and of Tony Powell's future wife, Violet, married the painter Henry Lamb in 1928.

70. Waugh, *Diaries*, 298–99.

71. Coghill to HY, 4 December 1928 (SY).
72. Ibid., n.d. [before Henry's marriage] (SY).
73. Interview with Sara Carr.
74. HY to Evelyn Waugh, 11 April 1929 (SY).
75. *Living*, 36.
76. Ibid.
77. Ibid., 133.
78. Ibid., 76. Links between *Living* and *The Waste Land* are explored by Giorgio Melchiori in *The Tightrope Walkers: Studies of Mannerism in Modern English Literature* (London: Routledge and Paul, 1956).
79. *Living*, 86.
80. Evelyn Waugh thought that this episode did not work. *Letters*, 35.
81. Coghill quoted these words back to Henry. Coghill to HY, 16 January 1928 (SY).
82. "A Novelist to his Readers: I," *Surviving*, 139.
83. See p. 52, and *Surviving*, 90–97.
84. Valentine Cunningham, *British Writers of the Thirties* (Oxford: Oxford University Press, 1988), 10. Stephen Spender thought that the young Auden had caught some of Green's style, and there may be an echo of it in Trudy's words at the beginning of *Paid on Both Sides*: "In Kettledale above Colefang road passes where high banks overhang dangerous from ambush. To Colefang had to go, would speak with Layard, Jerry and Hunter with him only." But he could equally have been responding independently to the same influences as Green.

    Rod Mengham relates the phenomenon observed by Cunningham to a lecture that Gertrude Stein gave at Oxford in 1926, "Composition as Explanation," and seeks to strengthen the link by saying that the lecture was published "by the Hogarth Press which was subsequently to publish *Living*." The main point is interesting, but *Living* was in fact published by Dent.
85. *Living*, 214.
86. Ibid., 229.
87. Ibid.
88. Ibid., 145.
89. Ibid., 73, 111.
90. Review of Virginia Woolf's *A Writer's Diary*, 1954, reprinted in *Surviving*, 179–83.
91. Frank Kermode, *The Genesis of Secrecy: On the Interpretation of Narrative* (London: Harvard University Press, 1979), 14.
92. From Friedrich Engels, *The Condition of the Working-Class in England* (1845), ed. and trans. W. O. Henderson and W. H. Chaloner (Oxford: Blackwell, 1971), 30–31.
93. *Living*, 78.

94. Ibid., 188.
95. Ibid.
96. Powell, *Infants of the Spring*, 198.
97. *Living*, 16.
98. *Surviving*, 51–58.
99. *Living*, 217–18.
100. HY to Lucy Byron, 19 January 1929 (Lucy Butler).
101. It was not the setting itself but Green's handling of his subject matter, of course, that was original. "The Great Drama of Factory Life" was one of the staples of romantic fiction in the early part of the century: See J. McAleer, *Popular Reading and Publishing in Britain, 1914–1950* (Oxford: Oxford University Press, 1992).
102. *Living*, 24–25.
103. HY to Anthony Powell, 13 October 1928 (SY).
104. Edward Garnett to HY (SY). See also George Jefferson, "Green and Garnett," *London Magazine,* June 1978, 53–62.
105. Quoted in Byron, *Letters Home*, 95.
106. HY to Margaret Byron, 29 October 1928 (Lucy Butler).
107. HY to Maud Yorke, November 1928 (SY).
108. Byron, *Letters Home*, 96.
109. It is still in her possession.
110. Byron, *Letters Home*, 96.
111. Margaret Byron to HY, 9 June 1929 (Lucy Butler).
112. HY to Anthony Powell, 12 November and 23 August 1928, and HY to Maud Yorke, 18 December 1928 (SY).
113. HY to Anthony Powell, 13 October 1928 (SY).

CHAPTER FIVE: *The Bright Young Yorkes*

1. HY to Margaret Byron, 1 January 1929 (Lucy Butler).
2. See *Surviving*, 28–47.
3. Constance's surname is Igtham (pronounced *Eyetam*)—a misspelling of Ightham, where Maurice Bowra's parents lived in Kent. Bowra had two younger sisters, Norah and Francesca. Bowra, *Memories*, 6, 58, 108.
4. *Surviving*, 45.
5. HY to Coghill, 5 December 1928 (EC).
6. Dent Records 11,043 (NC).
7. Interview with Anthony Powell.
8. HY to Robert Byron, n.d. (Lucy Butler).
9. HY to Waugh, 11 April 1929 (SY).
10. The details are set out in a letter to Vincent Yorke from John Biddulph dated 25 April 1929 (SY).

11. Bowra, *Memories,* 165.
12. Byron, *Letters Home,* 119, 2 May 1929.
13. HY to Lady Ottoline Morrell, 5 May 1929 (HR).
14. "Author's Work as Factory Hand," London *Star,* 15 June 1929.
15. HY to Waugh, 22 June 1929 (SY).
16. Interview with Lucy Butler; report in *The Times,* 26 July 1929.
17. HY to Maud Yorke, 9 August 1929 (SY).
18. He was persuaded to wear it again for a portrait by Matthew Smith. Russell, "There It Is," 433.
19. Dig Yorke to Maud Yorke, 15 September 1929 (SY).
20. Dig Yorke to Maud Yorke from the Grand Hôtel Canadel, Var, 5 August 1929 (SY); HY to Lady Ottoline Morrell from the Grand-Hotel et Hôtel des Bains, Bandol-sur-Mer, 1 September 1929 (HR).
21. HY to Lady Ottoline Morrell, 23 November 1929 (HR). The woman he appointed used to startle passing policemen by shouting up at them from the basement, "The days of rabbit pie are past, my man." Russell, "There It Is," 463.
22. The public dinner is described in a letter from HY to Lady Ottoline Morrell, 23 November 1929 (HR). The fancy-dress party had actually occurred a few months earlier: See *Sketch,* 3 July 1929.
23. Charlotte Mosley, ed., *The Letters of Nancy Mitford* (London: Hodder and Stoughton, 1993), 35, 23 January 1930.
24. Waugh, *Letters,* 66, 62. According to Diana Mosley (then Diana Guinness), Waugh used "bright young" for several of his more serious friends, such as "Bright young Roy Harrod." Diana Mosley, *A Life of Contrasts* (London: H. Hamilton, 1977), 79.
25. Interview with Anthony Powell.
26. Anthony Powell, *Hearing Secret Harmonies* (London: Heinemann, 1975), 54.
27. HY to Vincent Yorke, 21 May 1930 (SY).
28. In 1931, Evelyn Waugh told him, "I know what you must feel about your office. I have a corresponding longing for some kind of routine in my life." Waugh, *Letters,* 55. Later in the 1930s, after Henry had joined the Auxiliary Fire Service, he wrote, "Habit is what keeps me sane, the lack of it or break in it which nearly drove me mad when this wretched war began." HY to Mary Strickland, 25 November 1939 (Paul Bailey).
29. HY to Mary Strickland, 21 May 1935 (Paul Bailey).
30. Conversation with Sebastian Yorke.
31. Quoted in the *TLS,* 3 October 1929.
32. *The Station,* 1928, was followed in 1929 by *The Byzantine Achievement.*
33. Robert Byron to HY, 12 May [1929] (Lucy Butler). For Henry's *Cherwell* review, see pp. 274–75, n. 88.
34. *Life and Letters* 3 (July–December 1929): 66–67.

35. British *Vogue,* 3 September 1929, 43.

36. Waugh made this point in a letter to Henry dated June 1929, in which he also referred to the "telegraphic narrative," which he compared vividly if perhaps double-edgedly with "those aluminium ribbons one stamps out in railway stations on penny in the slot machines" (*Letters,* 35). Waugh later changed his mind about the style of *Living*—see below—but he was right first time. J. M. Synge famously wrote in the preface to *The Playboy of the Western World* that he "got more aid than any learning could have given me from a chink in the floor of the old Wicklow house where I was staying, that let me hear what was being said by the servant girls in the kitchen."

37. Stannard, *Waugh,* 1:224–25.

38. *Graphic,* 14 June 1930, 588, quoted in ibid.

39. Edward Garnett to HY, 7 May 1929 (SY). "I see that Gerald Gould was scandalized by 'Living' & your little tricks with the definite article. Poor mutt! Well you are punished for not making it easier to start with by inserting those 'descriptive' bits."

40. The reviewer was Dudley Carew, who had been a (somewhat subordinate) friend of Evelyn Waugh since their school days at Lancing.

41. R. N. Linscott, New York *Herald Tribune,* 11 August 1929. The piece was headed CINEMATOGRAPH. A good discussion of the book's filmic qualities is provided in Mengham, *Idiom of the Time,* 15.

42. HY to Lady Ottoline Morrell, 1 September 1929 (HR).

43. Ibid., 13 July 1929 (HR).

44. HY from 12 Radnor Place to Edward Garnett, 28 August 1931 (HR): "I have a genius here, a man called James Hanley. He was until a short time ago a docker & has since written books, which have been published in limited editions, about working men & has got everyone else cold the language he uses is so magnificent." Garnett thought the books "smelt of the lamp" but praised their freedom from political dogma (15 September 1931, SY). See also HY to Garnett, 9 and 15 September 1931, and HY to Lady Ottoline Morrell, 22 and 25 February 1933, all in HR.

45. Powell, *Messengers of Day,* 190.

46. Dent to HY, 11 January 1932 (NC).

47. HY to Guy Pocock, 16 January and 15 June 1932 (NC).

48. Ibid., 15 June 1932 (NC).

49. The trip is described in letters from Henry to his mother, 22 October and 16 November 1932 (SY).

50. Princess Martha Bibescu was to write a memoir of Proust, translated into English as *The Veiled Wanderer,* of which an unkind English reviewer said that a better title would have been *Du côté de la princesse* (*TLS,* 24 February 1950, 122).

51. The Guinnesses were struck by the fact that the Yorkes did not sleep in the

same room. Once, when the house was full of guests, Henry was so adamant about the impossibility of him and Dig sleeping together that a servant's room had to be made available for him (information from David Wolton). The Guinnesses also have an English country house at Biddesden, near Andover, and it was there that Bryan Guinness wrote his poem "Dirge" ("The rooks are blue, and the trees are brown, / And the farmer comes marching from over the down"), published in the *London Mercury* at Christmas 1932. He sent the poem to Henry, who commented in largely enthusiastic detail but persuaded his friend to make a change at the end, the original version of which, he felt, "wrecks the feeling." Bryan Guinness, *Pot Pourri from the Thirties* (Burford: Cygnet Press, 1982), 26–28.

52. HY to Edward Garnett, 15 September 1931 (HR).

53. Dig at Renvyle House Hotel, Renvyle, Connemara, Co. Galway to Maud Yorke, September 1933 (SY).

54. Waugh, *Diaries*, 325, 1–5 August 1930. One later visit has escaped Waugh's biographers. A practical joke was played on him one weekend by Mary Strickland's son Guy, who filled Waugh's overcoat pockets with silver teaspoons. The butler reported the loss of the spoons and later was startled to hear them clanking as he helped Waugh on with the coat as he left. Waugh demanded an apology but didn't get it. (Interview with Raymond and Sara Carr.)

55. In April 1937, Henry was best man at Waugh's second marriage, to Laura Herbert (Stannard, *Waugh*, 1:449).

56. Interview with Anthony Powell.

57. Ibid.

58. Interview with Sir Isaiah Berlin, see pp. 116–19.

59. Maurice Bowra was also a godfather. When Henry wrote to him telling him the date of the christening, he replied crustily, "Right. I shall be there & hope H.R.H. will not" (SY).

60. Interview with John Yorke.

61. Gerald Yorke, *China Changes* (London: Jonathan Cape, 1935), 249.

62. HY to Mary Strickland in South Africa, 30 December 1937 (Paul Bailey).

63. HY at the Hôtel Vouillemont, Paris, to Robert Byron, 31 March 1934 (Lucy Butler).

64. HY to Maud Yorke, 17 July 1935 (SY).

65. Ibid., 16 August 1935 (SY).

66. Sebastian Yorke relates that Henry became friendly with the boxer Jack Hood, "who trained for his fights with a one-legged publican called Wally Weston in the billiards room at Madresfield Court," the country home of the Lygons (*Surviving*, 293). In April 1934, Aly Khan wrote appreciatively from Paris in reply to a card Henry had sent. "Here I am missing all the good

in *Lettres nouvelles,* June/July 1953, 417–33, 550–65, and there was also an appreciation by Maurice Pons in *Revue de Paris,* 1956.

10. Welty, "Henry Green: A Novelist of the Imagination."

11. HY to Eudora Welty, 1 February 1961 (SY).

12. BBC-TV, *Bookstand,* 5 June 1962. The note stayed the same until his death eleven years later. Four months before he died, he talked to a *Guardian* journalist, Simon Blow: "I'm forgotten now. It's disappointing, but there it is. Nothing to be done about it" (quoted by Hancock, "Life of Henry Yorke," 103).

13. Letter read to the author by Terry Southern.

14. Dig Yorke to Carol Southern, n.d. (HR). The play was probably John Arden's *Live Like Pigs* (1958).

15. On a rare visit to Gerald and Angela at Forthampton, Henry wept over what he described as his lack of recognition. Angela recalled him saying, "I've never won any of the good prizes" (Paul Bailey).

16. Told by Gerald Yorke to Paul Bailey.

17. Gerald continued in this role for longer than a decade and also advised Allen and Unwin on what would now be called New Age publications. Many of the books were translations, which he spent long hours rewriting. According to his son John, when a book on Tibetan mysticism sold particularly well Gerald attributed its success to his choice of a cover design, which incorporated an archetypal symbol for the cry of orgasm; readers, he believed, chose the book subliminally.

18. In the BBC *Bookstand* interview, undertaken when he was still fifty-six, he described himself as "nearly sixty years of age." The following year, he told John Russell he was sixty (Russell, "There It Is," 445).

19. Having bruised his ribs falling against the wall of his cabin, he was looked after by a nurse who, he thought, had convinced herself that he was "the kind of romantic Englishman who slips quietly over the side and ends it all." Bruce Johnson, "A Note on Henry Green in Retirement," *Michigan Alumnus Quarterly Review* 66 (autumn 1960): 68–69.

20. Interview with Emma Tennant.

21. The word is used independently by Raymond Carr and Alan Ross, whose experiences of such spectacles would be hard to match.

22. Interview with Kitty Godley.

23. This story is told by Sebastian Yorke: *Surviving,* 296.

24. The visitor was Gerard Keenan.

25. Most of the stories in this paragraph were told to John Russell, "There It Is," 436ff.

26. *Surviving,* 297.

27. Ibid., 284.

28. Interview with Sir Raymond Carr.

29. Interview with Emma Tennant. In 1961, Green wrote about the barrier set up by religious novels to the irreligious: "I have just been reading Charles Williams, who to me is meaningless, and I have great difficulty with Antonia White, Graham Greene and the later Evelyn Waugh." In 1963, he said he didn't believe "in anything at all" (*Surviving,* 281, 284).
30. Russell, "There It Is," 460.
31. *A Little Learning,* 213.
32. The word literally means *tumbling down* but is less pejorative than *downfall.*
33. HY to Mary Strickland, 25 November 1966 (Paul Bailey).
34. The book was *The Colour of Rain,* published under the pseudonym Catherine Aydy. Tennant found Henry "less kind [about the novel] in person" when she visited him afterward at Wilton Place. He told her that she hadn't "really 'brought it off'" (*Girlitude,* 156).
35. Paul Bailey thinks that Dig brought these difficulties on herself through insensitivity. He recalls a lunch with her at which, as a long-suffering cook put steak and carrots on the table, Dig said to Bailey, "I don't know about you but I find carrots frightfully common."
36. HY to Eudora Welty, 25 February 1961 (SY).
37. HY to Terry and Carol Southern, n.d. (HR).
38. *Surviving,* 284.
39. Keene, *Two Mr. Smiths.*
40. *Surviving,* 279.
41. Dig Yorke to John Lehmann, n.d. (Princ).
42. John Lehmann to HY, 31 July 1971 (Princ).
43. Russell, "There It Is," 434.
44. Address delivered at the memorial service in Saint Paul's Knightsbridge, Wilton Place, 12 February 1974. A version was printed under the title "Henry Yorke, Henry Green" in *London Magazine* 14:2 (June–July 1974): 28.

SELECT BIBLIOGRAPHY
─────────

Works by Henry Green

GREEN'S BOOKS HAVE GONE IN AND OUT OF PRINT. A
few years after his death, they were all reissued, partly by the Hogarth
Press (*Blindness,* 1977, *Caught* and *Concluding,* 1978, *Pack My Bag* and
Back, 1979) and partly by Picador, which in 1978 published *Loving,*
Party Going, and *Living* in a compendium volume with an introduction
by John Updike, followed in 1979 by a similar collection of *Nothing,*
Doting, and *Blindness.* Both of these editions also appeared in the United
States, published by Penguin.

Since 1989, further reissues have kept Green's work in view. There
have been two editions of *Pack My Bag:* one from Oxford University
Press with an introduction by Alan Ross (1989) and another from Hogarth Press, introduced by Sebastian Yorke (1992, published in the
United States the following year by New Directions). As this book goes
to press, another edition of the memoir has come into view, along with
reissues of *Living, Loving,* and *Party Going,* all from Vintage. Meanwhile, Harvill Press has brought out all of the novels, starting with *Living* in 1991 and ending with *Doting* in 1998; *Surviving: The Uncollected
Writings of Henry Green,* edited by Matthew Yorke, was published by
Chatto and Windus in 1992 and by Viking the following year in the
United States; and Penguin (U.S.) also reissued the two earlier compendium volumes, the second of them with a new introduction, in 1993.

Because there is no standard edition, page references given in the text
and notes are to the first editions, which are listed below in alphabetical
order. Most of Green's short stories and articles can be found in *Surviv-*

ing, and in these cases, page references are to that volume rather than to the less accessible first publications.

Where I have had access to manuscripts, typescripts, or proofs, details are given in the relevant note.

BOOKS

Back, Hogarth, 1946
Blindness, Dent, 1926
Caught, Hogarth, 1943
Concluding, Hogarth, 1948
Doting, Hogarth, 1952
Living, Dent, 1929
Loving, Hogarth, 1945
Nothing, Hogarth, 1950
Pack My Bag, Hogarth, 1940
Party Going, Hogarth, 1939

SHORT STORIES, DIALOGUES, TRANSLATIONS, PLAYS

"Adventure in a Room," *Surviving,* 6–13
"Arcady, or A Night Out," *Surviving,* 26–27
"Bees," *Surviving,* 3–5
"Emma Ainley," *College Days* 8 (1923): 246–47
"Evening in Autumn," *Surviving,* 63
"Excursion," *Surviving,* 64–74
"Fight," *Surviving,* 59–62
"The Great I Eye," *Surviving,* 121–27
"The Jealous Man," *Surviving,* 174–78
"Journey Out of Spain," *Surviving,* 194–230
"The Lull," *Surviving,* 98–110
"Mr Jonas," *Surviving,* 83–89
"Monsta Monstrous," *Surviving,* 21–25
"Mood," *Surviving,* 28–47
"The Old Lady," *Surviving,* 111–14
"Olein," *Grand Street* 42 (1992): 42–45

"A Rescue," *Surviving*, 77–82

"Saturday," *Surviving*, 51–58

"Test Trial at Lords," *Surviving*, 48–50

"Their Son," *College Days* 7 (1922): 224–28

"The Waters of Nanterre," *Surviving*, 115–20

"The Wyndham Family," *Surviving*, 14–20

ARTICLES AND REVIEWS

"Apologia," *Surviving*, 90–97

"Before the Great Fire," *Surviving*, 260–79

"A Centaur," *Surviving*, 231–33

"The Complete Plain Words," *Surviving*, 184–87

"Edward Garnett," *Surviving*, 133–35

"The English Novel of the Future," *Contact* 1 (1950): 20–24

"Europe in the Looking Glass," *Cherwell*, 13 November 1926, 155

"Falling in Love," *Surviving*, 192–93

"A Fire, a Flood and the Price of Meat," *Surviving*, 151–57

"For Jenny with Affection from Henry Green," *Surviving*, 284–85

"For John Lehmann's Programme," *Surviving*, 163–65

"Henry Green," *Surviving*, 131–32

"Impenetrability," *Surviving*, 188–91

"Invocation to Venice," *Surviving*, 158–62

"Matthew Smith—A Personal Tribute," *Surviving*, 166–69

"A Novelist to His Readers: I," *Surviving*, 136–42

"A Novelist to His Readers: II," *Surviving*, 143–50

"A Private School in 1914," *Folios of New Writing* 1 (spring 1940): 11–25

"The Spoken Word as Written," *Surviving*, 170–73

"Too Little and Too Late," in *The Battle of the Books*, ed. Gerard Hopkins (London: Wingate, 1947)

"An Unfinished Novel," *Surviving*, 251–59

"Unloving," *Surviving*, 280–83

"A Writer's Diary," *Surviving*, 179–83

BOOKS, ARTICLES, AND DISSERTATIONS ON HENRY GREEN

Although the amount of critical writing on Green is small by comparison with that on some of his contemporaries, there is still a good deal of it. The critical works listed below are those that I have found most interesting. Fuller bibliographies can be found in the books by Rod Mengham and Oddvar Holmesland. Publication details of early reviews of and articles on Green's novels, as well as of biographical works that contain information about him, are given in the relevant endnotes.

Brooke Allen, "Reading Henry Green," *New Criterion,* March 1993, 61–68

John Ashbery, "Three Novels of Henry Green," unpublished paper written for the M.A. requirement, Columbia University, 1950

Leslie Brunetta, "England's Finest Hour and Henry Green's *Caught,*" *Sewanee Review* 100:1 (1992): 112–23

Andrew Gibson, "Henry Green as an Experimental Novelist," *Studies in the Novel* 16:2 (1984): 197–213

Michael Gorra, *The English Novel at Mid-Century,* Houndsmill: Macmillan, 1990, chap. 2, "Henry Green (1905–1973)," 21–57

Ann Hancock, "The Life of Henry Yorke and the Writing of Henry Green," Ph.D. diss., University of Warwick, 1981

Clive Hart, "The Structure and Technique of *Party Going,*" *Yearbook of English Studies* 1 (1971): 185–99

Oddvar Holmesland, *A Critical Introduction to Henry Green's Novels: The Living Vision,* New York: St. Martin's Press, 1986

Gerard Keenan, *The Professional, the Amateur, and the Other Thing: Essays from "The Honest Ulsterman,"* Belfast: HU Publications, 1995

Frank Kermode, "Green Fields, All Too Far Away," *Daily Telegraph,* 29 January 1977, 9

———. "The Chief Defect of Henry Green," *Daily Telegraph,* 12 February 1977, 11

———. "Still Green in the Memory," *Daily Telegraph,* 26 February 1977, 11

———. *The Genesis of Secrecy: On the Interpretation of Narrative,* Cambridge, Mass.: Harvard University Press, 1979

Rod Mengham, *The Idiom of the Time: The Writings of Henry Green,* Cambridge: Cambridge University Press, 1982

V. S. Pritchett, "The Future of Fiction," *New Writing and Daylight* 7 (1946): 75–81

———. "Back from the War," *The New York Times Book Review,* 1 October 1950, 4, 28

———. "Green on Doting," *The New Yorker,* 17 May 1952, 121–22, 125–26

Alan Ross, introduction to *Pack My Bag,* 1989

John Russell, *Henry Green: Nine Novels and an Unpacked Bag,* New Brunswick, N.J.: Rutgers University Press, 1960

Terry Southern (interviewer), "The Art of Fiction," *Surviving,* 234–50

Edward Stokes, *The Novels of Henry Green,* London: Hogarth Press, 1959

Julian Symons, "Doubting," *The Times Literary Supplement,* 23 June 1978, 695

D. S. Taylor, "Catalytic Rhetoric: Henry Green's Theory of the Modern Novel," *Criticism* (Detroit) 7 (1965): 81–99

John Updike, introduction to *Loving, Living,* and *Party Going* [one-volume reprint], 1978

———. Introduction to *Surviving* [see above]

Eudora Welty, "Henry Green: A Novelist of the Imagination," *Texas Quarterly* 4 (1961): 246–56

FURTHER ACKNOWLEDGMENTS

———

OVER THE YEARS, A LARGE NUMBER OF PEOPLE OTHER than those mentioned on pages ix–xii have helped me in my work on Green. Some of them were people who knew him and who talked to me about him: the late Mary Sanger-Davies, whose father was vicar of Forthampton in Henry's childhood; Reginald Hawkes, formerly the Biddulphs' butler; the late Lord Annan; the late Sir Isaiah Berlin; Gerard Keenan; Conan Nicholas; Pamela Nicholas; Jenny Rees; and John Russell. I am also grateful to the following for providing information or leads of various kinds or for answering queries: John Ashbery; Gerard Barrett; Patrick Bowe; Kate Bucknell; Carmen Callil; David Cannadine; Richard Davenport-Hines; Peter Davidson; Michael Davie and Anne Chisholm; Roy Foster; Tony Garrett; Oliver Gates; Mark Girouard; Victoria Glendinning; Warwick Gould; Sir Stuart Hampshire; Michael Holroyd; Samuel and Liz Hynes; Susannah Johnston; Julie Kavanagh; Francis King; John King; Hermione Lee; Edward Mendelson; Rosaleen Mulji; Bernard O'Donoghue; Peter Parker; Alexandra Pringle; Paul Rassam; Howard Rogovin; Malise Ruthven; Iain Sinclair; Iwan Sitniakowsky; Timothy d'Arch Smith; Ben Sonnenberg; Lucretia Stewart; John Stokes; Barbara Ann Taylor; Roger Thompson; David Tobin; Joseph Trapp; Fleur Treglown; Bradford Verter; Guido Waldman; Ann Waldron; George Wells; and David Wolton.

I HAVE BEEN HELPED BY MEMBERS OF THE STAFFS OF the following archives and institutions: the Harry Ransom Humanities Research Center of the University of Texas at Austin; the local-studies department of Birmingham Central Library; the BBC Written Archives

Centre; the Bodleian Library, Oxford; Bristol University Library; the British Library; the Brotherton Collection, Leeds University; the Cambridge University Archives; Eton College Library, especially its librarian Michael Meredith; Exeter College, Oxford; Guildhall Art Gallery; the Fire Service Division of the Home Office; the Harrods archive; the Imperial War Museum; l'Institut Français du Royaume-Uni; the library of the University of Iowa; King's College, Cambridge; the University of London Library; Magdalen College, Oxford; the Army Historical Branch, Ministry of Defense; the New Beacon School; the library of the University of North Carolina at Chapel Hill; the Centre for Oxfordshire Studies, Oxford Central Library; the Department of Rare Books and Special Collections, Firestone Library, Princeton University; the library of *Punch;* the library of the University of Reading and especially the keeper of its archives and manuscripts, Michael Bott; the Royal Society of Literature; Sevenoaks Public Library; the Society of Authors; the Theatre Museum; the archive of Time-Life; and Trinity College, Cambridge.

THE AUTHORSHIP OF COPYRIGHT MATERIALS FROM which extracts have been quoted is made clear either in the text or in the notes or both. Every attempt has been made to contact the literary estates concerned, and the author and publishers are particularly grateful to the following: Lucy Butler (for permission to quote from Robert Byron); Faber and Faber, Ltd. (W. H. Auden); the Estate of the late David Garnett (Edward Garnett, David Garnett); Her Grace the Duchess of Devonshire (Nancy Mitford); Greene and Heaton, Ltd. (William Sansom); David Higham Associates (John Lehmann, Louis MacNeice); Alice Keene (Mary Keene); the Provost and Scholars of King's College, Cambridge (G. H. W. Rylands); the Society of Authors (Rosamond Lehmann); Carol Southern (herself and Terry Southern); Lady Spender and Faber and Faber, Ltd. (Stephen Spender); Random House Archive and Library (Frank Swinnerton); A. P. Watt, Ltd. on behalf of The Lord Tweedsmuir and Jean, Lady Tweedsmuir (John Buchan); and Auberon Waugh (Evelyn Waugh).